it's time for thanksgiving

Books by Elizabeth Hough Sechrist and Janette Woolsey

IT'S TIME TO GIVE A PLAY

NEW PLAYS FOR RED LETTER DAYS

Books by Elizabeth Hough Sechrist

POEMS FOR RED LETTER DAYS

RED LETTER DAYS

ONE THOUSAND POEMS FOR CHILDREN

THIRTEEN GHOSTLY YARNS

HEIGH-HO FOR HALLOWEEN

CHRISTMAS EVERYWHERE

IT'S TIME FOR
THANKSGIVING

WRITTEN AND COMPILED BY

Elizabeth Hough Sechrist and Janette Woolsey

DECORATIONS BY GUY FRY

MACRAE SMITH COMPANY : PHILADELPHIA

Republished by Omnigraphics • Penobscot Building • Detroit • 1999

5710

SECOND PRINTING

Library of Congress Cataloging-in-Publication Data

Sechrist, Elizabeth Hough, 1903–
 It's time for Thanksgiving / written and compiled by Elizabeth
Hough Sechrist and Janette Woolsey ; decorations by Guy Fry.
  p. cm.
 Originally published: Philadelphia : Macrae Smith Co., 1957.
 Summary: Presents the history of Thanksgiving and its customs
together with stories, plays, poems, games, and recipes related to
the holiday.
 ISBN 0-7808-0307-8 (lib. bdg. : alk paper)
 1. Thanksgiving Day. [1. Thanksgiving Day. 2. Holidays.]
 I. Woolsey, Janette. II. Fry, Guy, ill. III. Title.
GT4975.S4 1999
394.2649 — dc21   99-28345
                  CIP

Printed in the United States

for

VERNON MONTGOMERY DODGE

and

ESTHER HOUGH HIBBERD

ACKNOWLEDGMENTS

The authors wish to express their thanks and appreciation to the following authors and publishers for their kind permission to include their works in this volume:

Beckley-Cardy Company and John Hoffman for "November's Gift" by Alice Crowell Hoffman from THE BIG BOOK FOR SPECIAL DAYS, published by Beckley-Cardy Company; Rowena Bennett and *Child Life* for four lines from "Thanksgiving Magic" from *Child Life Magazine,* copyright 1944; Carol Ryrie Brink and *Story Parade* for "Goody O'Grumpity"; Aileen Fisher and *Story Parade* for "Thanksgiving Blues"; Aileen Fisher and *Child Life* for "Thanksgiving Day In The Morning," from *Child Life Magazine,* copyright 1952; Aileen Fisher and *Jack and Jill* for "All In A Word," published in *Jack and Jill* under the title "Holiday Acrostic," reprinted by special permission from *Jack and Jill,* copyright 1952, by the Curtis Publishing Company; Dorothy Heiderstadt and *Child Life* for "Indians for Thanksgiving" from *Child Life Magazine;* J. B. Lippincott Company for "The Pilgrims Came" by Annette Wynne, reprinted with permission from DAYS AND DAYS by Annette Wynne, copyright 1919 by J. B. Lippincott Company; 1947 by Annette Wynne, published by J. B. Lippincott Company; McGraw-Hill Book Company, Inc. for "Child's Grace" from THE LITTLE WHISTLER by Frances Frost, published by Whittlesey House, copyright 1949, McGraw-Hill Book Company, Inc.; William R. Scott, Inc., and Dorothy Canfield Fisher for "A New Pioneer" from SOMETHING OLD SOMETHING NEW by Dorothy Canfield, published by W. R. Scott, Inc., copyrighted 1940 and 1949 by Dorothy Canfield; John C. Winston Company for "If I Were A Pilgrim Child" from STORY-TELLER POEMS by Rowena Bennett and used by permission of the publisher, The John C. Winston Company.

contents

history

stories

plays

poems

CONTENTS

games

8

CONTENTS

recipes

RECIPES FOR THANKSGIVING GOODIES

by Elizabeth Hough Sechrist

9

CONTENTS

it's time for thanksgiving

THE HISTORY OF THANKSGIVING

the first thanksgiving

ELIZABETH HOUGH SECHRIST

E veryone knows the first Thanksgiving in America was in the new little colony of Plymouth, in what is now the state of Massachusetts. But we must start in England to go back to the very beginning of our Thanksgiving holiday. In the town of Austerfield in the year 1590 a son was born to the Bradfords and they named him William. This boy was to grow up to become the Governor of the tiny Pilgrim colony of Plymouth, established in 1620 along the rough shores of the New World.

When William Bradford was still a youth, he came under the influence of William Brewster. Through him he became interested in a church group in Scrooby which held its meetings in secret. The accepted church of the government was what is now known as the Church of England. However, many of the people held beliefs that differed from those of the official church. Such was the case in William Bradford's group. The members felt that, even though they might become involved with the English law, they must worship God in their own way. And so their meetings were held in secret places without the knowledge of the authorities. But some of the people did get into trouble with those who enforced the law, and some were thrown into jail.

Now these were peace-loving folk and they had no desire to

break the law. But still they felt that, above all, they must follow their consciences in the matter of their worship of God. And so they began to talk among themselves of leaving their home country of England where they had spent all their lives. They planned to go to Holland. Now two of the leaders of this plan were William Bradford and William Brewster. Carefully they made preparations for their group—men, women and children—to emigrate. And eventually, in 1608, that plan was carried out for most of them. But William Bradford was put under arrest and sent to prison before he could escape with his friends. When he had served his prison sentence, however, he was able to join the others.

In Holland a man could worship as he pleased. The Dutch people were peace-loving and kind. But the families who had children worried about bringing up their boys and girls in a manner that was foreign to their own upbringing. And so, after twelve years of living in a strange country where the customs were so different from their own, the Pilgrims came to a most unusual and daring decision. They determined to cross the Atlantic Ocean and go to the New World! After many disappointments and several false starts, they finally made the long and treacherous voyage to America on the *Mayflower*. They landed at last on the rock-bound shores of a strange and lonely coast. And they named the land New England.

Many books have been written about that brave band of people who landed in Plymouth on that cold December day in 1620; of their terrible hardships, of their heavy loss of members who died, of the bravery and determination of those who survived. It is a part of our American history of which we can all be proud.

The Pilgrims themselves were grateful in that autumn of 1621. In spite of all their many difficulties, they had survived as a colony. In less than one year from the date of their arrival their gratitude led them to hold a time of Thanksgiving.

With the death of John Carver, first governor of the colony, William Bradford was chosen to take his place. He was only thirty-one years old, but he was wise and brave. He had known sorrow in the loss of his young wife soon after they had reached the new

16

land. But Governor Bradford was thankful to God for the blessings that had come to his group at the close of this first year. It seemed to him that a special day should be set apart for showing thanks. In way of celebration they would have a feast! When he spoke of this to others, his idea must have been received with enthusiasm. Elder Brewster suggested that they should share their good fortune with the friendly Indians. And so an invitation was sent to Chief Massasoit urging him and others of his tribe to come and join with them.

It must have been a busy and exciting time for the women and girls who prepared the food for the celebration. Four marksmen had been sent out to kill meat for the occasion and they had come back laden with wild turkeys, quail and other game. All this meat had to be prepared and cooked, to say nothing of a quantity of shellfish and eels, bread, greens, berries and plums. Cooking facilities were of the crudest. Pots and pans, such as there were, probably had to be filled many many times. But the hands of those who prepared the feast were willing and quick. The delicate odors from the outdoor roasting and boiling and stewing that continued for days, must surely have filled the people of that little colony with anticipation for the great day to arrive!

But at last it did arrive, and with it, soon after dawn, came Massasoit and ninety of his fellow tribesmen. If the Pilgrims were surprised to see so many Indians appear in answer to their invitation, they made no sign. Elder Brewster conducted a service of prayer, just as always, before food was eaten by these reverent people. The strangers looked on quietly while the Pilgrims prayed. Long plank tables had been set up under the trees. The food, in great abundance, was placed upon the tables and the feast began.

In the satisfaction of being able to eat all they wanted at that first feast, there was probably not much time given over to conversation. But there must have been some talk among them. No one knows what words were exchanged as they sat about the long tables in the chilly December air. But we might imagine that some of the remarks may have gone like this:

Elder Brewster: Almighty God hath surely blessed us. One cannot help but think of our present situation and compare it with the hardships of our first winter in this place.

Captain Miles Standish: Aye, and to think that we have such an abundance of food that we may eat without worry for the morrow!

Governor Bradford: There is no need for anxiety this year about rations for the winter. Our crops were excellent. The harvest was good, and as a result we have ample food stored away for the year ahead.

Elder Brewster: It was the Lord's goodness that sent the sun and rain in proper proportions to make our crops grow.

Governor Bradford: That is right, Elder Brewster. Twenty acres of corn we put in, and six of wheat, barley and peas. Though our peas grew only to wither on the vine, we have had a goodly supply of other foods to take their place. I am sure that each and every one in our colony of more than fifty men, women and children is grateful to our Heavenly Father this day.

Elder Brewster (As he looks smiling at the people busily eating): Aye, and all seem to be enjoying the good food our womenfolk have prepared for our Thanksgiving feast.

Captain Standish: And those others are enjoying the food, too— the Indians and their chief, Massasoit. It would seem to me, my friends, that this day of sharing with our Indian neighbors will not be forgotten by them. Our people will want and need the good will of the red men. Perhaps today has impressed them with our sincere desire to live with them in peace.

If these were not the exact words spoken by the three principal men of the Plymouth Colony that day, we know at least that they were in their thoughts. And we know that the sincere wish of the colonists to be friends with the Indians *was* understood. History tells us that Massasoit was always willing to live in peace with his neighbors in the Plymouth Colony. As a matter of fact, an act of friendship occurred at this first Thanksgiving feast when Massasoit sent several of his best hunters into the forest to shoot five deer for the Pilgrims. One of the deer was roasted and eaten at the festival which lasted three days. The other animals were dressed and stored away against the wintry snow-filled days when wild game would become scarce.

And so the first Thanksgiving in the New World which occurred on a day in December, 1621, was a successful occasion. To Americans all over this vast nation now, more than three hundred years later, the very fact that the Pilgrims established Thanksgiving Day makes us grateful to them.

a history of thanksgiving customs

ELIZABETH HOUGH SECHRIST

When the first Thanksgiving was observed by the Pilgrims of the Plymouth Colony, they little dreamed that the day would ever become a national holiday. In this strange new land where they had settled and known great hardships, the Pilgrims felt deep gratitude to God for the blessings that had come to them, and they wished to show their thankfulness. The first Thanksgiving observance was in December, 1621. On July 30, 1623, Governor Bradford proclaimed a second Thanksgiving when a ship was sighted, heading for port carrying sorely-needed supplies from England. This second Thanksgiving Day was not in any way connected with the harvest, but later on a day *was* set in the month of

November which became associated with the ingathering of the crops. In the year 1668, with the appointment of November 25th as Thanksgiving Day, these words were written into the Plymouth Colony Records:

> "It has pleased God in some comfortable measure to bless us in the fruits of the earth."

In celebrating the harvest the Pilgrims were following a custom that had been observed in one way or another by different races and peoples for many centuries. In their own native land of England, harvest-time had been observed in rural sections for many years. When the last crop was brought in and the country people celebrated the event, they sang this song:

> "Harvest home, harvest home,
> We have ploughed, we have sowed;
> We have reaped, we have mowed;
> We have brought home every load;
> Hip, hip, hip! Harvest home!"

Eventually the separate harvest celebrations of each farm were combined in a community observance, with all the people of the parish taking part. The master or squire held a big feast and sat down at the same table with his servants and all the farmers of the parish and their wives and children. This custom of feasting and sharing was probably well-known to the Pilgrims and influenced them in their desire to hold a Thanksgiving feast.

The harvest was not the only reason the British had for holding Thanksgiving days. Throughout English history there were days set apart to commemorate some special blessing or deliverance. Only sixteen years before the Plymouth Colony's Thanksgiving, a day had been proclaimed in England "in grateful deliverance" of the Gunpowder Plot. A man by the name of Guy Fawkes had hatched a plot to blow up the Houses of Parliament, seat of the British Government. But fortunately his plot was discovered and prevented, and the infamous Guy Fawkes was hanged. The uncovering of the plot was on November 5, 1605.

20

There were other Thanksgiving days besides those on the English calendar that may have been an inspiration to the Pilgrims for their own observance. It must be remembered that these religious refugees from England had lived for twelve years in Holland. There they had seen the Dutch people annually observe a Thanks-

giving day in October to commemorate their victory over Spain in the year 1575.

Another influence may have come from the American Indians. We know that the Indians were accustomed to observing several days of Thanksgiving throughout the year. The Iroquois, for instance, had an autumn festival known as the Green Corn Dance which lasted three days. We are familiar with the story of how the Indians came to the first Thanksgiving feast at the invitation of the Pilgrims. Accounts of that occasion tell us that Massasoit, who was Chief of the Wampanoag tribe, of the Algonquins, came with his ninety warriors to the feast and remained with their new white friends three days. It seems likely that a three-day period of Thanksgiving was customary for them.

The idea of celebrating the harvest is very old. In ancient Greece there was the Feast of Demeter, a nine-day celebration in honor of Demeter, Goddess of the Harvest. In Rome it was Ceres who was similarly honored with an Ingathering Festival. Even the pagan Druids of ancient Britain held harvest ceremonies in the fall of the year.

But the oldest harvest festival known to us is that of Succoth, the Jewish Feast of the Tabernacles. It occurs in the autumn—in the Jewish Calendar, Tishri fifteenth. After the tribes of Israel left Egypt they wandered for a period of forty years before reaching the Promised Land. During this time they lived in lattice huts, small shelters erected on the desert sands. After they had reached the Promised Land they wished to show gratitude to God for their deliverance. And so, in order that they would not forget their wanderings of those troubled years, they chose a most unusual way of commemoration. Each year they lived in small huts for a period of seven days. During that time they prayed and feasted and gave joyful thanks to God for their blessings.

The Feast of the Tabernacles, or Ingathering as it is sometimes called, is still observed today by the Jewish people. In the modern manner, each family builds a *succa*, a small hut or shelter on the side of the house, in which the Holy Ark is placed. In countries outside of Israel the Succoth is observed for nine days. The eighth day of Succoth is known as the Solemn Assembly. On the last day, the conclusion of the nine-day observance, there is a celebration of the Rejoicing of the Law. The Scrolls of the Law are removed from the Holy Ark in a ritual in which a procession is made seven times around the *succa*. To the people of the Jewish faith, their ancient harvest festival is a time not only for being thankful, but for helping others less fortunate than themselves.

Harvest or Ingathering Feasts have been known for hundreds of years in the agricultural sections of Lithuania, Poland, Czechoslovakia and other European countries. In Norway, though not a holiday like our Thanksgiving, the day is a time of happy celebration among the country people. It is known as *Höst Gilde* or, literally, the Golden Harvest.

In Russia, in the olden days, the harvest festival was a time looked forward to eagerly by the peasants. Before the young people began their fun on that occasion, they first observed a solemn ritual to bring good luck to the household. All who had assembled to join in the festivities would walk slowly toward the house carry-

ing wreaths, which had been prepared earlier, made of wheat, rye, barley and oats woven together. The old wreath from the year before was taken down from the side of the house and the new one hung in its place. Then there was a feast of good things for all. After that came the dancing, the most popular part of the celebration. The young people were familiar with every part of the folk dance, known as the *khorovod*, which tells the entire story of the harvest routine.

The Festival of the Harvest Moon has been celebrated in China for centuries. According to the lunar calendar used by the Chinese, the harvest moon reaches fullness on the Fifteenth-day of the Eighth Moon (month). This day is also known as the Moon's Birthday. All over China housewives prepare for the holiday by baking "moon cakes." Even though the cakes are intended for the Moon Queen, the Chinese boys and girls devour them with great relish. And they are not surprised to see the figure of a rabbit traced on the top of their cakes. They have been told from babyhood that (instead of a man-in-the-moon) it is a rabbit who lives there and whose features they see in the shadows of the moon when it is full.

23

In Canada Thanksgiving day is usually observed on the second Monday in October.

It took many years for Thanksgiving Day in America to become the permanent and regularly observed holiday we know today. The New England Colonies observed it from time to time. As early as 1644 in the New Amsterdam Colony, in what is now the city of New York, the governor of that settlement on the Hudson river issued a proclamation calling for a day of Thanksgiving. In 1784, because the American colonists were so grateful that the Revolutionary War was ended, a special Thanksgiving day was observed. Five years later, in 1789, President George Washington issued the first Thanksgiving Proclamation of the new nation, the United States of America. That proclamation included these words:

> "Now therefore I do recommend and assign Thursday the twenty-sixth day of November next to be devoted by the People of these States to the service of that great and glorious Being . . . That we may then all unite in rendering unto him our sincere and humble thanks for his kind care and protection of the People of this country previous to their becoming a Nation, for the single and manifold mercies . . . which we experienced in the course and conclusion of the late war, for the great tranquility, union, and plenty, which we have enjoyed . . . and in general for all the great and various favors which he hath been pleased to confer upon us."

It must have seemed an appropriate thing to the people of the new nation to set aside a day for giving thanks for all their blessings, just as the Pilgrims had 168 years before. The war with the British was over, and their colonies, now states, were at last united. In 1795 another Thanksgiving day was set by President Washington. Then, in the year 1815, President James Madison proclaimed a Thanksgiving day because of the close of the War of 1812.

After 1815 a national Thanksgiving day as such became almost unknown. Some of the states observed it by proclamations of the governors of their respective states. But the observance was mostly irregular, varying in the date from state to state. It is said that at one time virtually every state observed Thanksgiving day on a different date. It was as though this struggling new feast-day lacked enough support to become really established in the country where it had seen its birth. That is, until Mrs. Sara Josepha Hale began to support it.

Mrs. Hale has often been called the Mother of Thanksgiving Day, for it was by her constant efforts the holiday came into its own. For years she had worked toward getting national support to make Thanksgiving Day a real "national holiday the same as Fourth of July." When she became editor of *Godey's Lady's Book* in 1846, she was able to take her message straight into the homes. The circulation of this popular magazine for women was large, and at last her cause was heard by the multitudes. But Mrs. Hale did not stop here. She wrote thousands of letters rounding up those who could help along the cause. She sent letters to the governors of the states urging them to make Thanksgiving an annual holiday in their states. She even wrote to the President, Abraham Lincoln, sending him a copy of Washington's original Thanksgiving Proclamation of 1789. Finally she was rewarded with an interview in which she and the President discussed this movement which was so close to her heart. The result of that interview came in 1863 when President Lincoln made the last Thursday in November an annual, national Thanksgiving Day. In his Proclamation, he said, in part:

> "The year that is drawing to a close has been filled with the blessings of fruitful skies . . . It has seemed to me fit and proper that they should be solemnly, reverently and gratefully acknowledged as with one heart and one voice by the American people."

The persistence and untiring efforts of one woman had resulted in a national legal holiday that not only the women of America but all in the home could take to their hearts.

The custom since 1863 has been for the President to issue a

proclamation setting the day of Thanksgiving for the District of Columbia and the Territories and Possessions of the United States. This is followed by similar proclamations by the governors of all the states. The national day has been the fourth Thursday in November almost without exception. However, on those occasions when there have been five Thursdays in November, some of the New England states have chosen to celebrate the last Thursday. Another exception was in the years 1939 and 1940 when President Franklin D. Roosevelt called upon the nation to observe the third Thursday in November. Some states objected to the extent that in 1941 the date of Thanksgiving was again different in different states. So in 1941 a joint resolution of Congress provided:

> "That the fourth Thursday of November in each year after the year 1941 be known as Thanksgiving Day, and it is hereby made a legal public holiday to all intents and purposes."

Our American Thanksgiving is the first such holiday in the world to become a legal holiday. We can see from this account how it started and how it grew. It is truly a family day and, aside from Christmas and Easter, the only national holiday in our calendar with religious significance. Perhaps, more than any other day of the whole year, it is a day when we can be thankful to God the Great Provider for all that America means to us.

STORIES ABOUT THANKSGIVING

the pumpkin pie procession

ELIZABETH HOUGH SECHRIST

When Mistress Satterthwaite heard that their old friend Christopher Ludwig was ill, and that he and his wife needed her, she made plans to go to them at once, good woman that she was. At first she thought she would take Baby Betsy with her. But then she decided against it, for fear her two-year-old daughter would disturb the sick man. "And besides," she told her eldest daughter, "thee is fifteen, Lydia, and well able to look after Betsy and the others."

"And I shall be able to look in upon them now and then," said Father.

Father Satterthwaite was so easy-going, and so absent-minded at times, that his wife doubted his supervision would be of much account. But his printing shop was only a short distance from the house, and he could look in on the children now and then.

But all of Mother's anxiety was wasted, for on her first day at the Ludwigs' nothing at all out of the ordinary happened at home. That evening when Father drove the two miles out to the Ludwig place and fetched her home, he had a good report to make.

"The children are all fine," he said, as though she had been away for weeks. "Our Lydia is quite a little woman, and Deborah, for all her tender age of eleven years, is almost as grown up."

29

"Father, Deborah is twelve! And how did the boys behave?"

"I am sure they were not behaving in an unseemly way when I was home for dinner. In fact, thee has nothing at all to concern thyself with, wife. And I am sure thee will find a hearty supper has been prepared by the girls when we reach home."

Father was right. Lydia had supper all ready to dish up. Deborah had set the table, Betsy met them at the door dressed in a dainty pinafore, and the boys, Jonathan and Alfred, were waiting with clean hands and faces.

"Now I declare," Mother said as she removed her bonnet. "This is real cozy. And I am tired and hungry, so let us eat at once."

While they were eating the children launched into an account of how their day had passed.

"I am glad thee were all so good," their mother said.

"Well, Mother, Alfred wasn't very good," Deborah began, giving her brother a dark glance.

Lydia interrupted quickly. "Alfred was all right, Debbie. Thee knows as long as he has that drum in this house thee is going to have to hear him play it."

"It nearly drives me crazy!" said Deborah. "If he drums all day tomorrow I shall just have to go along with Mother. Mother, how is Master Ludwig?"

"Master Ludwig is very much better, but still confined to his bed. And, being better, he is worrying about his customers."

"What is happening to his bakery business since he is not able to bake?" asked her husband.

"Mistress Ludwig is doing the baking; that is why she needs me to look after her husband. And as thee knows, Father, Master Ludwig is not the most patient man in the world. My goodness, if I had not reminded myself that he is really a very fine gentleman at heart, I should have lost my temper more than once today at his complaining. He worries constantly about his customers, and I am sure his wife is doing the very best she knows how. It takes her all day and much of the evening to prepare and bake the bread and rolls. Naturally, their customers cannot expect them to bake cakes and pies too."

30

"It is natural for a man to worry about his business," Father put in.

"Master Ludwig has so much pride that he cannot reconcile himself easily to disappointing anyone. That's why he was so upset today about the pumpkin pies."

"What about the pies?" they asked.

"Two of his best customers ordered large pumpkin pies and he is not able to bake them, and his wife has not the time."

"Well, now that's something I could do for Master Ludwig!" said Lydia as she began to remove the plates. "I can make good pastry, as thee well knows, Mother. Couldn't I make the pies tomorrow? Then thee could take them to him on Wednesday."

"We shall see," was all her mother said. "Anyway, I do hope Master Ludwig is in a better frame of mind tomorrow."

"Just because he was—something or other in the Army, he's pretty vain, I think," said Jonathan.

"He was Baker General of the Army of the Revolution, appointed by General Washington, now *President* Washington," Father explained patiently.

"He says he is the best baker in the United States," Alfred told them.

"And I am sure he is that," spoke up Mother. "And now, after my difficult day with the Baker General, I am going to bed."

The next morning in the hurry of getting Mistress Satterthwaite off, Lydia almost forgot about the recipe for the pumpkin pie. But she reminded her while her mother was tying her bonnet strings.

"Is thee sure thee wants to try it, my dear? Thee can make good pie crust, I know, but it is not so easy to make pumpkin pies. The pumpkin has to be cut up and cooked just right, and thee must be very careful to have the oven not too hot for the custard."

"Yes, I know, Mother. But do tell me quickly about the ingredients."

"Oh dear! Thy father is waiting for me. Well, just remember, Lydia, thee must use a cup of milk and one egg to each cup of mashed pumpkin. And to that thee must add the sugar and spices. Listen carefully, for we have not time to write it down."

31

While Lydia and Deborah listened attentively, she named the ingredients and the quantities to use.

"We'll remember," they assured her.

"Then send thy brothers to the market for the pumpkin. And now I must be going. Good-by, my Baby Betsy. Be a good girl for thy sisters." She kissed little Betsy and then turned to her two sons. "Go now for the pumpkin," she told them.

All five children followed their mother to the door so they could wave to her. Getting into the carriage she called to them at the last moment. "Remember, two large ones!"

The children waved from the doorway.

"Two pumpkins," said Lydia, turning to Alfred and Jonathan. "And go at once, for it will soon be time for thee to go to school."

The two boys ran down the street toward the market and Deborah followed her sister into the house.

"Sister, with all thee has to do this day it seems to me I should stay home from school to help thee."

Lydia shook her head. "Mother would not like it," she said. "And besides, I am sure I can manage nicely alone."

Deborah sighed as she helped her sister to remove the breakfast dishes from the table. "I miss all the fun by going to school," she said.

Lydia was washing the dishes when Deborah called her a few minutes later. "Come quickly, Lydia!"

Lydia joined her sister at the window in time to see Jonathan and Alfred coming down the street rolling two immense pumpkins, pumpkins so big they could not possibly have carried them.

"Mercy on us!" exclaimed Lydia, and she opened the door to help them get the pumpkins inside. "What on earth did thee get such big ones for?"

"Mother said two large ones," Jonathan replied. "These are the largest they had."

"I don't doubt it for a moment! The largest in all Pennsylvania, or I miss my guess," their sister declared.

Deborah looked at the huge yellow pumpkins. Then she looked at Lydia. "Lydia, is thee sure thee can manage alone?"

Lydia looked at the pumpkins too, and then smiled. "Thee wins, Deborah. I shall need thee, and even with thy help this will require a bit of doing!"

The boys went off to school, Betsy was set in a sunny corner of the room with her beads to play with, and the two girls set to work immediately, cutting into one of the pumpkins. They cut and pared, and pared and cut. As soon as there was enough prepared to fill the big black kettle, Lydia set it to cooking over the fire.

"When that's cooked enough to be mashed I'll have all the other ingredients ready," said Lydia. And she began measuring out sugar and milk and spices. Deborah kept on paring and cutting pumpkin.

"I may as well start to make the pastry too," Lydia said.

The stuff in the kettle simmered, then boiled merrily while they worked. Lydia kept testing it to see if it were tender. At last she announced that it was cooked enough. And now came her first surprise.

"There seems to be a great deal of pumpkin here," she said as she mashed the yellow pulp. "Yes, a *great* deal of pumpkin!"

"And plenty more here," said Deborah, who was still cutting up the first pumpkin. "To say nothing of that other great big fellow sitting there!"

"Well," said Lydia cheerfully, "I have plenty of milk and eggs, since it is still so early in the week."

She began to measure the pumpkin mash. With each cupful she

33

added a cupful of milk and an egg. Three, four, five, six, seven—ten cupfuls of mash. Ten cups of milk, ten eggs. Sugar, brown and white. Spices. "Does that sound right?" she asked Deborah.

"Yes, I'm sure it is. But oh, Lydia, so much! Does thee expect to need so much filling for thy pies?"

"Now, Deborah, don't worry, child. I am only following Mother's instructions."

She began pouring the golden filling into her pastry-lined pie plates. Five large pies went into the oven. "My goodness, I'll need to make more crust to go with all this filling that is left over," she said.

"Thee had better put the rest of this pumpkin on to cook, meanwhile," said Deborah.

"Well, that's sensible. While the pies are baking the pumpkin can be cooking, and I, meanwhile, shall be making more pastry." Suddenly she laughed. "This must be somewhat like running a bakery, Debbie. Does thee not think so?"

"Perhaps. But if my job were to do the cutting of the pumpkin day in and day out, I should have no hands left!" As she spoke she rubbed her sore fingers together.

By the time Father and the two boys came home to dinner there were five beautiful pies cooling on the deep window sills in the kitchen. And there were five more baking in the oven, and a large kettle of pumpkin cooking over the fire. Lydia hastily cleared off the table so that they could eat.

"Bread and cheese and coffee is all thee gets today, and this!" Lydia told them as she placed one of the golden pies in the center of the table.

The pie, they all agreed, was delicious. "We have a fine baker in the family," Father told her as he ate his second piece.

After he and the boys had left, Lydia removed the big kettle of pumpkin from the crane and put it to one side of the hearth to cool.

"We still have a great deal to do, Debbie," Lydia told her sister. "But first I must hurry over to Mistress Allen's and ask to borrow her pie plates and kettle. Perhaps she can let me have some milk, too. Thee had better rock Betsy to sleep while I am gone."

When Lydia returned carrying a basket of pie plates and a kettle full of milk, Betsy was fast asleep on the settee. Deborah was cleaning up the dinner dishes.

"Perhaps I could make pies while thee cuts the pumpkin, Lydia," she said hopefully.

"I'm sorry, but thee must cut the pumpkin. 'Never shirk a duty, however unpleasant,' our mother always says!"

"If I must, I must, I suppose!" And poor Deborah went back to her cutting. "Does thee realize that thee has baked ten pies, and there is another kettle of cooked pumpkin, and that much of the pumpkin is still to be cut?"

"Hush, dear. I am counting. One, two, three cups milk. Three eggs. I'm so glad Mistress Allen could loan me her kettle."

For a long time no word was spoken in the big Satterthwaite kitchen. The girls did not wish to disturb their little sister, for a Betsy sleeping was far easier to look after than a Betsy running about. Lydia had removed another batch of pies from the oven. She hoisted the neighbor's big kettle up to the crane, its large black interior crammed with cut-up pumpkin. She poked at the fire and then put more wood on it. Then she worked fast with her rolling-pin to prepare the pie crust.

"I just simply cannot seem to keep abreast of the filling with enough pastry!" she exclaimed, for the first time sounding tired and a little bit cross.

"Here, let me roll the dough for thee for a spell," said Deborah. "I am so tired of cutting and paring that I think my fingers will fall off."

"Well, I must mix more pastry," said Lydia, "but I believe we shall have to borrow some flour. And when Mother sees how low the lard has got in the lard can, I fear she'll be displeased."

A little while later the two boys came home from school, and before the girls could caution them, they had wakened Betsy with the noise of drumming and fife-playing.

"Now see here!" Lydia scolded. "As busy as we are we can't have thee making matters worse! Jonathan, sit down here and cut these pumpkin pieces into slices! And Alfred, thee can go over to Mistress Allen's and borrow a basin of flour."

"I am no girl to do cooking chores," Jonathan protested.

"And I am no girl to go a-borrowing, either!" Alfred exclaimed, and went on with his drumming harder than ever.

"Do as Lydia says!" commanded Deborah.

"Oh, so thee thinks thee can dictate to us since Mother is away," said Jonathan unpleasantly.

It looked like a family row. Lydia was about to shoo the two boys out of the house when suddenly there was a dreadful clatter, and screams that rose above the banging of Alfred's drum. Betsy had pulled over the kettle of cooked pumpkin that stood by the hearth, and the children's surprise turned to terror as they thought of the hot soupy mixture, and how it might scald her severely. They all rushed to her. Fortunately the pumpkin had cooled to a moderate temperature, and Betsy's worst casualty was fear. She screamed at the top of her lungs while Lydia hastily picked her up and tried to wipe the yellow gooey mess from her face. Betsy was bathed in pumpkin. It was in her eyes and ears and down her neck. Her curly hair was sticky with it. And her bare feet were oozing yellow from every pore.

"Thank fortune, she's not hurt," Lydia breathed with relief. "Just frightened."

Just at that moment the door opened and Father came in. He saw Betsy in Lydia's arms all streaked and dirty; the upturned kettle with pumpkin spilled on hearth and floor; the mess of cooking pots and pie plates and flour and other ingredients covering the table; and pies baked and unbaked in every available place that Lydia and Deborah could put them. He hesitated before he spoke, as though uncertain how to take all this.

"Is the child hurt?" he asked at last.

"Oh, no, Father," Lydia assured him in a shaky voice. "She is only frightened. She—she fell into the pumpkin."

He heaved a deep sigh and looked about the room again. "All I can say, children, is that thee had better get this place cleaned up before thy mother comes home."

Turning on his heel he went out.

Lydia set the weeping Betsy on her feet. "Now, Betsy, thee is all right. Here, let me wash thy face. Jonathan, sit thee down and slice up that pumpkin without more ado. Alfred, go to Mistress Allen's house and borrow some flour. Deborah, clean up the floor as best thee can until the pies are done, then we'll make a better job of it. As for myself, I must get finished with the pies!"

The others had met with Lydia's determination before this, and they knew from experience that it would do them no good to protest. They all did as she told them, and soon the room was buzzing with activity again. Jonathan cut pumpkin; Deborah rolled out pie dough; Lydia filled pies and put them in to bake. But Alfred came back with only a cupful of flour.

"Mistress Allen has only this much flour, but her sister Mistress Howard was there when I called, and she has gone to her house to fetch some. She'll be over with it presently," Alfred said.

Before long there was a knock at the door. It was Mistress Howard with the flour. She looked about the disorderly kitchen with interest. "It's very good of thee to help out Master Ludwig with his baking," she said.

After she had left another knock sounded.

"I heard thee is baking for poor, ill Master Ludwig," said another neighbor. "I brought thee some milk."

37

"Thee is very kind," Lydia said, accepting the pitcher. Before she could close the door another donor appeared on the steps.

"We have heard of thy kindness to Master Ludwig and we thought thee might be able to use a dozen eggs."

Lydia thanked the woman and carried the milk and eggs into the house. "How word does get around! Alfred, stand near the door and if anyone else comes, thee must do the honors, for we dare not leave our baking."

And Alfred was kept busy, for a fourth neighbor came, and a fifth. But it was growing late in the afternoon when old Master Trumbull came bringing his offering. Lydia was just putting the last batch of pies into the oven when she heard Alfred talking to him.

"Oh, we thank thee, Master Trumbull. It is very generous of thee." He closed the door and turned around facing the others. "Look what Master Trumbull has brought us!" he called out triumphantly, and walked toward them carrying a large pumpkin.

"Oh no! Not another pumpkin!" Lydia exclaimed.

Suddenly they were all doubled up with laughter. The kitchen was hot and steamy from the cooking, and filled with the odor of boiled pumpkin and baked pumpkin and spices and pie crust that had gone into the making of innumerable pumpkin pies! Lydia's hands and face and clothing were smudged with flour and yellow streaks of mashed pumpkin! And her fingers were blistered and sore from baking pumpkin pies. And her arms and back ached, and her feet hurt from tearing around the kitchen all day long. And her sister Deborah was not in much better condition. Supper was not started, and the house was a mess, and their mother was due home soon. But here was another pumpkin!

As tired as they were, the girls sat down and laughed hysterically.

"If anyone ever says pumpkin pie to me again I think I shall die!" choked Deborah, wiping the tears from her eyes.

"Well, we can't just sit here," said practical Lydia. "Mother and Father will be here before we've had time to clean up."

Lydia was like a whirlwind again, giving orders and pitching in herself with all her usual vigor. The pots and pans and bowls and dishes were washed and put away. The big wooden table was scoured and scrubbed until it shone. The plank floor of the kitchen was given the same treatment. Deborah gave the sticky Betsy a bath while Lydia cut vegetables into a meat broth and set it to simmering over the fire. Then the two girls made themselves presentable while the clock on the mantel ticked on to six o'clock.

When their parents came in, the scene that met their eyes was one they always liked to see in their home. The two boys were amusing Betsy with a fife and drum concert. The soup was hot in the kettle, the table was set with a clean cloth, and everything in the room bespoke cheerfulness. The children had agreed not to mention the pies until the subject was brought up by one of the parents.

"My, it looks so cozy and warm and cheerful in here!" their mother said, removing her bonnet and cloak. "And everything looks so clean!" She gave Betsy a kiss. "Why, thee has even washed Betsy's hair."

Betsy put her hand to her head. "Punking in hair!" she said, but her mother didn't seem to hear.

"Thee must have had a very busy day," went on Mother, "for thy father tells me thee made the two pumpkin pies for Master Ludwig."

"Did thee say *two* pies, Mother?" asked Lydia in a strange voice. And Deborah repeated, *"Two pies?"*

"Well, if thee has made only one it is no matter. He can choose which customer shall have it."

At that all the children began to laugh. *"Two pies!"* screamed Jonathan.

Mother spoke to him sharply. "Now, Jonathan Satterthwaite, if there is anything to laugh about, perhaps thee had better share the joke!"

By way of answer, Lydia opened the cupboard door and showed her the rows of pies on the shelves. Then she led her to the pantry and showed her more pumpkin pies. And lastly, she opened the door to the seldom-used parlor and showed her pumpkin pies on the marble-topped table, on the deep window sills, and on the mantel shelf. Mother looked at the pies, then looked at the girls. She was speechless. They went back into the kitchen where Mother dropped weakly on the settee.

Finally she asked, "How many?"

"Eighteen!" said Lydia and Deborah in unison.

"But why?"

"We thought thee said two large pumpkins," they told her.

"But thee must have said two large pies!" exclaimed the boys.

"Punkings. Punking pies!" piped up Betsy.

Then Mother began to laugh. She laughed until the tears had to be wiped away. It seemed as though no one could stop laughing until Father said, "But what are we to do with so many pies?"

And then Mother said, "Oh! Oh dear! That's the funniest, and the strangest, part of all!"

"What does thee mean, strangest?" they wanted to know.

"Just this. Yesterday word reached Philadelphia that President Washington has issued a proclamation that this Thursday—day after tomorrow—is to be Thanksgiving Day. And when the message was brought here to Germantown today and Master Ludwig heard it, he was filled with dismay."

"He was?" said Father.

"Yes, indeed he was. He said, 'Our President wants us to celebrate Thanksgiving Day. And here am I, one-time Baker General

40

of the Army, sick in bed and unable to make even one pumpkin pie. And everybody will want pumpkin pie for Thanksgiving.' "

"Pies? If it's pumpkin pies he wants!" shouted Lydia. "Oh, Mother, thee has surely brought good news tonight. Deborah, we have found good use for our eighteen pies. And a reason for all of our back-breaking work of this terrible day!"

"But how shall we ever get so many pies to Master Ludwig?" asked Deborah practically.

"There is only one safe way to carry an open-faced custard pie," said Mother, "and that is to carry it in one's hands."

And that is how the Procession of Pumpkin Pies came to happen on the day before Thanksgiving in the village of Germantown. Word spread quickly through the neighborhood, and the good friends and neighbors of the Satterthwaites came to the rescue. At an agreed time a dozen or more young people and some of the parents showed up at the Satterthwaite house. And when the signal was given the procession from there to the Ludwig house two miles away, began. Leading the parade were Alfred with his drum and Jonathan and another boy with their fifes. They played "Yankee Doodle" in such a merry and fetching manner that all who heard them picked up the air and sang it too. And many of them joined the procession, though they knew not whither it was bound. Eighteen pie-bearers followed the fife and drum corps, all walking carefully so as not to spill the pumpkin pies which must be delivered in good condition to Master Ludwig. "Yankee Doodle went to town, a-riding on his pony!" they sang.

And if ever there was before, or ever will be again such a strange procession through the streets of old Germantown, no one can remember it. But in 1789 some very strange things could have happened, and neither thee nor I should doubt it.

a new pioneer

DOROTHY CANFIELD FISHER

A new girl came into the Winthrop Avenue public school about the beginning of November. This is how she looked to the other boys and girls in the seventh grade. She couldn't understand English, although she could read it enough to get her lessons. (This was a small public school in a small inland American town where they seldom saw any foreigners, so people who couldn't speak English seemed outlandish.) She wore the queerest-looking clothes you ever saw, and clumping shoes and great, thick, woolen stockings. (All the children in that town, as in most American towns, dressed exactly like everybody else, because their mothers mostly bought their clothes at Benning and Davis' department store on Main Street.) Her hair wasn't bobbed. It wasn't curled. It was neither a long nor short bob; it looked as though her folks hadn't ever had sense enough to bob it. It was done up in two funny-looking pigtails. She had a queer expression on her face, like nothing anybody had ever seen—kind of a smile and yet kind of offish. She couldn't see the point of wisecracks but she laughed over things that weren't funny a bit, like the way a cheer-leader waves his arms. She got her lessons *terribly* well (the others thought somebody at home must help her more than the teachers like), and she was the dumbest thing about games—didn't even know how to play run-sheep-run. And queerest of all, she wore *aprons!* Can you beat it!

That's how she looked to the school. This is how the school looked to her. They had come a long way, she and her grandfather, from the town in Austria where he had had a shop in which he repaired clocks and sold trinkets which the peasant boys bought for their sweethearts.

Men in uniforms and big boots had come suddenly one day—it was in vacation and Magda was there—and had smashed in the windows of the shop and the showcase with the pretty things in it. They had thrown out all the furniture from Magda's home back of the shop and made a bonfire of it in the street. Even though Grandfather had not said a word to them, they had knocked him down and hit him with their sticks till his white hair was all wet with scarlet blood. Magda had been hiding in a corner and saw this. Even now, she sometimes saw it all again and woke up with a scream, but Grandfather always came quickly to say smilingly, "All right, Magda child. We're safe in America with Uncle Harry. Go to sleep again."

He had said she must not tell anybody about that day. "We can do something better in the New World than sow more hate," he said seriously. She was to forget about it if she could, and about the long journey afterwards, when they were so frightened, and had so little to eat; or, worst of all, when the man in the uniform in New York thought for a minute that something was wrong with their precious papers, and they might have to go back. She tried not to think of it, but it was in the back of her mind as she went to school every day, like the black cloth jewelers put down on their counters to make their pretty gold and silver things shine more. The American school (really a rather ugly old brick building) was made of gold and silver, shining against what she was trying to forget.

How kind the teachers were! Why, they *smiled* at the children. And how free and safe the children all acted! Magda simply loved the sound of their chatter on the playground, loud and gay and not afraid even when the teacher stepped out for something. She did wish she could understand what they were saying. She had studied English in her Austrian school, but this swift birdlike twittering didn't sound a bit like the printed words on the page. Still, as the days went by she began to catch a word here and there, short ones like "down" and "run" and "back." And she soon found out what *hurrah!* means, for the Winthrop Avenue School made a specialty of mass cheering and every grade had a cheer-leader, even the first-graders. Magda thought nearly everything in America was as odd and funny as it was nice. But the cheer-leaders were the funniest with their bendings to one side and the other, and then jumping up straight in the air till both feet were off the ground. She loved to yell, "Hurrah!" too, although she couldn't understand what they were cheering about.

It seemed to her that the English language was like a thick heavy curtain, hanging down between her and her new schoolmates. At first she couldn't see a thing through it. But little by little it began to have thinner spots in it. She could catch a glimpse here and there of what they were saying, when they sometimes stood in a group, looking at her and talking among themselves. How splendid it would be, she thought, to have the curtain down so she'd really understand what they were saying!

This is what they were saying—at least the six or seven girls who tagged after Betty Woodworth. Most of the seventh-graders were too busy studying and racing around at recess time to pay much attention to the queer new girl. But some did. They used to say, "My goodness, look at that dress! It looks like her grandmother's—if she's got one."

"Of all the dumb clucks. She doesn't even know enough to play squat tag. My goodness, the first-graders can play *tag*."

"My father told my mother this morning that he didn't know why *our* country should take in all the disagreeable folks that other countries can't stand any more."

"She's Jewish. She must be. Everybody that comes from Europe now is Jewish. We don't want our town all filled up with Jews!"

"My Uncle Peter saw where it said in the paper we ought to keep them out."

Magda could just catch a word or two, "country" and "enough" and "uncle." But it wouldn't be long now till she could understand everything they said, and really belong to seventh grade.

About two weeks after Magda came to school Thanksgiving Day was due. She had never heard of Thanksgiving Day, but since the story was all written out in her history book she soon found out what it meant. She thought it was perfectly lovely! She read the story of the Pilgrim Fathers and their long hard trip across the ocean (she knew something about that trip) and their terrible first winter, and the kind Indian whose language they couldn't understand, who taught them how to cultivate the fields, and then,—oh, it was poetry, just *poetry*—the setting aside of a day forever and forever, every year, to be thankful that they could stay in America! How could people (as some of the people who wrote the German textbooks did) say that Americans didn't care about anything but making money? Why here, more than three hundred years after that day, this whole school, and every other school, everywhere all over the country, was turning itself upside down with joy that their great-grandfathers had been brave enough to come to wild, uncivilized America and stick it out rather than put up with the bad treatment they were getting in Europe. (Magda knew something about that, too.)

Everybody in school was to do something for the celebration. The first-graders had funny little Indian clothes, and they were going to pretend to show the second-graders (all dressed up like Puritans) how to plant corn. Magda thought they were delightful, those darling little things, being taught already to be thankful that they could go on living in America. Some grades had songs, others were going to act in short plays. The children in Magda's own seventh grade that she loved so, were going to speak pieces and sing. She had an idea all her own, and because she couldn't be sure of saying the right words in English she wrote a note to the teacher about it. She would like to write a thankful prayer (she could write English pretty well now), and learn it by heart and say it, as her part of the celebration. The teacher, who was terrifically busy with a bunch of boys who were to build a small "pretend" log cabin on the stage, nodded that it would be all right. So Magda went away happily to write it and learn it by heart.

"Kind of nervy, if you ask me, that little Jew girl horning in on *our* celebration," said Betty.

"Who asked her to come to America, anyhow?"

"I thought Thanksgiving was for *Americans!*"

Magda, listening hard, caught the word "American" and her face lighted up. It wouldn't be long now, she thought, before she could understand.

No, no, they weren't specially bad children, no more than you or I—they had heard older people talking like that—and they gabbled along, thoughtlessly, the way we are all apt to, repeating what we hear, without considering whether it is right or not.

On Thanksgiving Day a lot of these grown-ups, whose kind of talk Betty and her gang had been repeating, had come, as they always did, to the "exercises." They sat in rows in the assembly room saying "the first-graders are too darling," and "how time flies," and "can you believe it that Betty is up to my shoulder now, seems like last week she was in the kindergarten?"

The tall principal stood at one side of the platform and read off the different numbers from a list. By and by he said, "We shall now hear a prayer written by Magda Bensheim, and spoken by her. Magda has been in this country only five weeks."

Magda came out to the middle of the platform, a bright, striped apron over her thick woolen dress, her braids tied with red ribbons. Her heart was beating fast. Her face was shining and solemn. She put her hands together and lifted them up over her head and said to God, "Oh, thank you, thank you, dear God, for letting me come to America and nowhere else, when Grandfather and I were driven from our home. I learn out of my history book that Americans all came to this country just how Grandfather and I come, because Europe treat them wrong and bad. Every year they gather like this—to remember their brave grandfathers who came here so long ago and stay on, although they had such hard times. American hearts are so faithful and true that they forget never how they were all refugees, too, and must thankful be that from refugees they come to be American citizens. So thanks to you, dear, dear God, for letting Grandfather and me come to live in a country where they have this beautiful once-a-year Thanksgiving, for having come afraid from Europe to be here free and safe. I, too, feel the same beautiful thank-you-God, that all we Americans say here today."

46

Magda did not know what is usually said in English at the end of a prayer, so she did not say anything when she finished, just walked away back where the other girls of her class were. But the Principal said it for her—after he had given his nose a good blow and wiped his eyes. He looked out over the people in the audience and said in a loud, strong voice, "Amen! I say Amen, and so does every-body here, I know."

And then—it was sort of queer to applaud a prayer—they all began to clap their hands loudly.

Back in the seventh-grade room the teacher was saying, "Well, children, that's all. See you next Monday. Don't eat too much turkey." But Betty jumped up and said, "Wait a minute, Miss Turner. Wait a minute, kids. I want to lead a cheer. All ready? Three cheers for Magda!"

"Hip! Hip!"—she leaned 'way over to one side and touched the floor and they all shouted "Hurray!"

She jumped straight up till both feet were off the ground and clapped her hands over her head and "Hurrah!" they all shouted.

The wonderful moment had come. The curtain that had shut Magda off from her schoolmates had gone. "Oh! Ach!" she cried, her eyes wide, "why, I understood every word. Yes, now I can understand American!"

47

the thanksgiving goose

ELIZABETH HOUGH SECHRIST

Aunt Cora has always preferred goose to turkey," said Grandma as she helped herself to more applesauce.

The two little boys looked at her with alarm in their faces. It quickly changed to dismay when Grandpa said, "That reminds me, I'm going to kill that sassy Chinese gander for Thanksgiving this year. Tomorrow, in fact."

"Not Francis?" Lewis and Jeddie exclaimed together.

"Of course we'll have turkey besides," Mother said, trying not to notice the look on the boys' faces.

They were eating supper in the big farm kitchen. There were Grandfather, Grandmother, Father, Mother, the two boys and Cherry, their little sister. It was only two days until Thanksgiving and the family had been discussing plans for the holiday. Aunt Cora and Uncle Tom were coming to spend the day with them.

"Grandpa, you just mustn't kill Francis!" Lewis said, his voice a wail.

Grandma snorted. "Francis! What a ridiculous name for a goose!"

"I love Francis," said Jeddie. "He eats corn right out of my hand, nice as anything!"

"I love Francis too!" said Cherry, pounding her spoon on the table for emphasis.

"He's a consarned bossy pest, that's what he is," said Grandpa. "Why, only today he was fighting again. He's always picking on the younger geese. He's a big bully."

"But he doesn't mean any harm, Grandpa," said Lewis. "Daddy says he's cross because he lost his mate."

Jeddie appealed to his father. "Daddy, don't you let Grandpa

48

kill Francis. He eats corn right out of my hand. And he's too tough to eat. Isn't he too tough, Daddy? Isn't he?"

But Father wasn't much comfort. "He's your Grandfather's goose, Jeddie. You mustn't argue with Grandpa."

"There's no argument," Grandpa said emphatically. "It's the chopping-block for Mr. Gander, and the other fowls will be better off without him."

At this Jeddie began to cry. He ran around the table to his mother and hid his head in her lap. Cherry set up a lusty howl in sympathy, and to add to the din the parrot from her cage began squawking in her shrill voice at the top of her lungs.

"Consarn it! I'm going out to do the milking." And Grandpa left the table, grabbed up his lantern and disappeared out the back door.

Mother tried to console Jeddie. Grandmother stuffed a cookie into Cherry's mouth to distract her. Father jumped up and threw a cover over Polly's cage to stop her squawking.

Meanwhile Lewis was looking down at his plate dismally, thinking of Francis' awful fate. A tear rolled down his cheek and dropped into his dish of applesauce.

"Now, see here, you boys," said Father sternly. "Your grandfather is tired of catering to that infernal goose. Francis *is* a bully. I heartily agree with Grandpa that the very best place to put that fat meddlesome bird is in the oven and on the Thanksgiving table."

Jeddie raised a tearful face. "But we l-love Francis."

"I'm sorry about that, Jeddie. I honestly am. You'll just have to realize that when you live on a farm there are bound to be some—er—some sad partings in store for you if you make friends with the animals."

Lewis thought for a moment. "You couldn't kill Jocko, Daddy, and *he's* a farm animal."

"Lewis, we don't eat donkeys. We do eat geese." He rose from the table. "Now, let's not talk about it any more."

When Father had gone outdoors to help Grandfather, the three children gathered around Mother. Grandmother started clearing away the dishes.

"Will Grandpa really do it, Mother?" asked Jeddie mournfully.

"I'm afraid so, Jeddie."

Lewis said fiercely, "All because of Aunt Cora! I *hate* Aunt Cora!" With that he rushed from the room and ran upstairs.

He was soon joined by Jeddie who told him that Mother said he must come downstairs and apologize for saying such a dreadful thing about Aunt Cora.

"Well, okay," said Lewis in a resigned voice. "I know I shouldn't have said it, but—Say, Jeddie, can't you think of some way we can save Francis?"

"No, I wish I could. Why don't *you* think of something, Lewis?"

"Well, I have thought of one way we might save him. We might hide Francis so Grandpa couldn't find him. But that wouldn't do."

"Why not?" Jeddie wanted to know.

"It wouldn't be honest, and Grandpa would get awful mad if he couldn't find him."

"Oh gosh! Then what are we going to do?"

Lewis shook his head solemnly. "I don't know, Jeddie. The worst of it is, we haven't much time. He'll kill Francis tomorrow because the next day is Thanksgiving."

While the boys were upstairs in their room talking, Mother and Grandmother were busy in the kitchen starting their preparations for the Thanksgiving Day feast. But Mother found time to cook up a batch of molasses candy for the children. She went to the foot of the stairs and called the boys.

"Lewis, if you and Jeddie would come down and shell the peanuts, it would help me with this molasses candy I'm making."

It didn't take long for the boys to put in an appearance, and Cherry was there already, running from one cooking pot to another begging for tastes. Lewis went and stood in front of his grand-mother.

"I'm sorry I said that about Aunt Cora."

"Your Aunt Cora is very fond of you, Lewis," said Grandma.

"I know. I don't really hate her. I was mad!"

"Yes, I know," said Grandmother. "And we're sorry the goose has got to be killed. But I dare say that when you've tasted that delicious goose all brown and—"

Jeddie interrupted, stamping his foot angrily. "Grandma! Don't you say that! We won't eat a bite of Francis!"

"Come, boys, get busy with the peanuts," Mother said. She put a large bowl of peanuts on the table and spread out a newspaper for the shells. "My, these look good. Here, Cherry, you climb up on this chair and you can help too."

So peace was restored and for a while the only sounds in the room were the cracking of peanuts and the bubbling of things in the kettles on the stove. But Lewis's next remark to his mother showed where his thoughts had been all the while.

"Mother, I've thought of something. Why couldn't Grandpa sell Francis to someone who wants a good lively gander? Then we could buy a goose at the market for Thanksgiving."

His mother had been stirring the molasses mixture. She stopped her stirring and dropped a spoonful of the hot syrup into a saucer of cold water.

"It's done," she announced.

Grandma quickly buttered a large platter and the boys dumped the bowl of shelled peanuts onto the platter. The odor of the candy as Mother poured it over the peanuts was almost enough to distract Lewis from his question. But not quite.

"Couldn't we, Mother? Couldn't we do that?"

His mother looked at him sadly and shook her head. "I do declare, Lewis, you have a one-track mind. Son, I do wish you could stop thinking of that goose. And you know that Daddy asked us not to talk about it."

So for the remainder of the evening nobody talked about Francis. As to what they thought, that was a different matter. And

51

the thoughts of the two boys were concentrated on the hope that some strange and wonderful miracle would happen to save their friend from the chopping-block.

When the children woke up next morning they were delighted to see a light covering of snow on the ground. But their pleasure was soon dampened when they remembered that this was to be the fateful day for their pet gander.

While they were eating breakfast Grandfather came into the kitchen.

"If you boys will be ready in twenty minutes I'll take you into town with me. The belt on the saw motor is broken, and Jim Burns is here to help your father to work on the new stalls in the barn."

The boys were delighted. "We're ready now, Grandpa!" said Lewis, and Jeddie jumped up from the table with his toast in his hand, exclaiming, "Oh boy! We're going to town with Grandpa."

It was always a treat to go into town. Grandpa never failed to stop at the drugstore, giving each of the boys a dime to spend any way they wished. Usually they bought ice cream cones. But sometimes Jeddie bought a new ball or toy. Lewis's sweet tooth always won out in his decision, and even now as he and Jeddie ran out to the barnyard to wait for Grandpa to get out the old truck, he could taste the sweets he planned to buy.

Almost without thinking the boys wandered over to the small pond which lay east of the barn. Most of the ducks and geese were standing restlessly in groups near the water, waiting for their breakfast of corn.

"There's Francis!" shouted Jeddie, and he and Lewis crossed the planks which formed a boardwalk over the marshy ground. It was from this point that the ducks and geese were always fed. When the boys began walking toward them, the ducks set up a loud clatter, closing in and looking for corn. Francis, who had been busily pecking in the mud looking for bugs, came hurriedly, half running, half flying toward them. The sun gleamed on his white feathers. He stretched his long neck out to its full length, then drew it in; stretched it out and drew it in with excitement.

Lewis put one hand in the pocket of his blue jeans.

"Shucks, Francis, I've only got one or two kernels of corn in my pocket."

"I've got some, Francis," said Jeddie. "Here, boy!"

Jeddie always had corn in his pockets. He held out his hand and Francis, unafraid, came close to the boy and, with staccato movements of his sharp bill, found the yellow kernels. Lewis stood by, looking on sadly, his eyes misted with tears.

"Gosh," was all he could say.

The two stood motionless while Francis made a business of probing into their pockets for more corn.

Just then Mother and Cherry appeared. Mother had an old bucket filled with corn. Cherry carried her own small pail, filled to the brim. Soon the mallards and 'scovies were crowding about them, pushing each other in their haste to eat the corn that was tossed to them. But the geese were always more reticent. With quiet dignity they waited until their share was thrown in their direction. That is, all but Francis. He nearly crawled into Jeddie's arms trying to get the corn away from him.

"Isn't he a mess?" laughed Jeddie, pushing the gander away from him, then holding out his palm so Francis could eat from it. "Look, Mother, just see how he eats from my hand, like it was a plate!"

Mother nodded and smiled but said nothing, perhaps because she found a lump in her throat. And just then the pick-up truck came noisily around the side of the barn and Grandfather called to the boys. They both threw generous handfuls of corn in Francis' direction and ran toward the car.

"At least he's safe until we get back," Lewis whispered.

Mother and Cherry waved after the car until it disappeared up the road.

"Cherry, why don't you finish feeding the ducks and geese for me," her mother said. "I'll go up and feed the chickens."

Cherry agreed, and she began by throwing fistfuls of corn in every direction. "It goes down into the snow, Mother," she complained.

"Go and stand under the tree, honey, where the ground is dryer,"

Mother suggested. Under the big walnut tree in the field, a little beyond the pond, there was a place bare of snow. So, as her mother had suggested, Cherry proceeded to feed the big birds from there. Her mother went on to the chicken house to finish her feeding chores.

Francis, as usual, pushed the other ducks and geese rudely out of his way while he ate the largest share.

"You piggy, you!" Cherry scolded. Then she stood for a moment contemplating him. In a different and softer tone then she said, "Poor Francis. Poor, poor Francis!"

For another minute she watched him eat. It would have been hard to guess what was going on in the little girl's mind. She looked all about her and suddenly started to walk away from the tree. Dropping corn and calling to Francis she kept on until she had come to the fence at the edge of the field. Here she found what she had evidently been looking for. Close to the fence there was an old wooden crate lying on its side. The hinged top was missing and some of the slats were broken. It had probably been discarded and forgotten by everyone but Cherry. Cherry remembered it because she had used it often to stand on when she wanted to climb the fence. Now she could think of another use for it.

The space beside the crate seemed to Cherry a good place to put all the rest of her corn. She emptied it in a heap, and Francis rushed greedily upon the kernels. Cherry was watching. There was the crate, and there was Francis, so close to it. She moved quietly until she stood directly behind the wooden box. A little shove; it moved. Francis was very busy eating and noticed nothing. Another little shove. Then a big push, and the crate went over.

It was nearly two hours later that Grandfather and the boys returned. Grandfather went to the barn while Lewis and Jeddie ran immediately to find Mother.

"Mother, come see what we bought!" Lewis shouted excitedly. But he need not have shouted for Mother was right there in the kitchen with Grandmother, baking pies for the morrow. Cherry, as usual, was at their heels.

Lewis opened a paper bag and brought out two small candles

54

which he placed on the table. They were in the form of Pilgrims, one a Pilgrim man holding a musket, the other a little Pilgrim lady in gray and white dress and bonnet, her hands clasped piously before her. They all exclaimed with pleasure, while the boys stood by beaming with satisfaction at their purchase.

"They're for you and Grandmother," Lewis said.

"Well, I never!" Grandma exclaimed with pleasure.

"They're just as cute as they can be," Mother said, picking up the candles to examine them more closely. "We'll put them on the Thanksgiving table, won't we, Grandma?"

Grandma said yes, they certainly would. And she gave both boys a hug, and a special one for Lewis because she knew what a sacrifice it must have been for him to forego the usual sweets.

"Did you have a good time with Grandpa?" Mother asked as she went back to rolling pastry on a floured board.

"Oh sure!" Jeddie answered promptly. "We stopped at the Wilsons and Grandpa bought a great big live turkey gobbler, for Thanksgiving dinner."

At the mention of the turkey a shadow crossed Lewis's face and he went over to the window and stood looking out. After a moment he turned and said crossly, "That turkey's big enough to feed an army! I don't see why we've got to have goose too!"

Just at that moment the door opened and Grandpa entered the kitchen.

"Well, Jim Burns fixed the saw. He and the children's daddy have a good day's work ahead of them to finish before dark." He turned to Grandma. "Grandma, how about pouring me a nice hot cup of coffee, and then I'll go out and chop—" He checked himself, looking quickly at the boys. "We brought home a nice fat turkey," he continued. "You'd better put a big kettle of water on the stove." No one said a word. Grandpa now turned to Mother.

"Say, how about letting the boys shell those mixed nuts we bought at the store for your nut cake? Cherry will help too, won't you, baby?"

Mother said the boys could shell the nuts, and as soon as the pies were in the oven she would make the nut cake. She looked questioningly at Grandpa as she talked, and he nodded back at her. Mother and Grandma knew that Grandpa was going to take care of more than the turkey. And the boys knew it, too.

After Grandpa had drunk his coffee he went out. Lewis, from the window, saw him stop at the tool shed and emerge with the ax. He turned about, clenching his fists.

"I guess Grandpa thinks we're little kids not to know he's going to chop Francis' head off!" he exclaimed.

"Lewis," said his mother sternly, "you are the eldest and I think you should set a good example for the younger ones by accepting what has to be."

Lewis cast his eyes downward and made no answer. Jeddie looked from one to the other, then started to run for the back door. "I won't let him! I won't let him kill Francis!" he cried, and pulled open the door. But Mother called to him sharply, and bade him come back.

"Now I want you all to be sensible!" Then, her eyes falling on the little Pilgrim candles, she said, "Remember how the Pilgrims killed turkeys and other wild things for their Thanksgiving dinner? Grandma, suppose you tell the children the story of the first Thanksgiving, and we can look at the little Pilgrim candles and try to imagine just how it must have been."

Cherry seemed to be the only one interested in the story Grandma began to tell, and she hung onto every word with great satisfaction.

But Grandma hadn't got very far when she was interrupted by Grandpa who came storming into the house looking very angry.

"Where's that infernal gander?" he shouted, addressing the two boys.

They looked at him in genuine surprise.

"Where did you hide him? Speak up, now."

"We—we didn't hide him, Grandpa," Jeddie avowed.

"Is Francis gone?" Lewis asked hopefully.

"I don't know how far he's gone, but I'll warrant you boys do!" And Grandfather glared at them. Then he turned to Mother. "They're your young 'uns. Tell them to go out there and find that goose so I can get this business over with and get back to my other work."

But Mother's face wore a puzzled frown as she said, "I don't understand, Papa. The boys couldn't have hidden Francis because he was out there with Cherry and me when the boys left with you. And they came into the house as soon as you returned. No, Grandpa. The boys haven't hidden the goose. He was out there with the others when Cherry finished feeding them."

" 'Deed he was, Grandpa!" piped up Cherry.

Grandpa scratched his head in a puzzled fashion. "I don't understand," he said. "That goose wouldn't have flown away because his wings are clipped. He just must be out there somewhere. Well, come on, boys. Help me to find him."

"I'll help too," said Cherry, going for her coat. The boys and Cherry ran outside with Grandpa. They looked everywhere, or so they thought. The boys even walked through the marshy ground surrounding the pond, looking through the high grass, and calling Francis' name. When they returned Cherry was standing on the wooden boardwalk where she had been watching them. When the boys drew near she began to laugh.

"What are you laughing at, silly?" asked Lewis.

"Don't you wish you knew, don't you wish you knew," she sang in her most provoking manner. But the boys paid no attention to her and presently she went back to the house to help Mother and Grandma with the pies and cakes.

57

By supper time Grandpa was so annoyed and upset that he forbade anyone to mention the gander's name. The turkey had been plucked and dressed, and as soon as the supper dishes were done Mother sat down to make the stuffing. The boys had left to go on a private search of their own for their pet. Cherry was curled up on the settee, half asleep.

"I declare, Mother," whispered Cherry's mother, "I just can't figure out what could have happened to Francis."

"Look," said Grandma softly. "Cherry is smiling in her sleep. I guess she's dreaming about Thanksgiving."

Everybody was up bright and early on Thanksgiving Day, for there were still many things to be done. The turkey was put into the oven at an early hour. By twelve o'clock the smells that filled the kitchen were almost too wonderful to be borne. The table was set with two extra places and the little Pilgrims were placed in the center, one on either side of a bowl of late yellow chrysanthemums.

At precisely twelve-thirty Uncle Tom's sedan drove into the yard. Everyone ran to the kitchen door to greet the guests. As they entered, Aunt Cora sniffed the air expressively.

"Mmm! I never smelled anything so good in all my life. I do believe it smells like goose."

Before anyone could reply to this remark Uncle Tom turned to Grandpa and said, "By the way, Father, what's going on up in the field?"

"Eh? Where?"

"Why, up along the fence, at the edge of the field. As we came down the road we could see the ducks raising a great clatter about something. They've all left the pond and are crowded together up there as though something had gotten after them. Maybe it's a fox."

The men and boys didn't lose any time getting out to the field to see what was the matter. Cherry, as soon as she could get into her coat, followed after them.

They could see as they came closer that the ducks, instead of being frightened, were assembled like an interested crowd watching a parade. Their eyes were centered on something that looked like a dancing box. Now, there is nothing more curious than a duck, and as his curiosity mounts his excitement rises. They were grouped about an old crate, jostling and pushing each other to get a closer look. Grandpa and the others edged in closer too, and then

they saw that the crate was moving and pushing about as though possessed. There was only one conclusion to make.

"There's something inside that crate!" Father shouted. He waded through the ducks and gave the crate a push, and there before their astounded eyes was Francis!

"Francis!" shrieked Jeddie, running toward the gander.

But Francis was very angry. His feathers were ruffled and dirty. With an angry honk he half flew, half ran away from them as fast as he could go.

"Now how did that goose get under that box," remarked Uncle Tom in wonderment.

"How long do you suppose he was under there?" asked Father.

"I think the boys can answer all those questions," Grandpa said in a stern voice.

"Lewis and Jeddie, did you hide Francis?"

The boys looked straight at their father. "Honest, we didn't," they said.

There was tense silence for a moment and, by the expression on

59

Grandpa's face, it seemed as though this Thanksgiving Day was doomed to be an unhappy one.

"I did it! I saved Francis. I love Francis."

They all turned to look at Cherry, and even as she spoke she ran over to the crate and showed them how she had pushed it over Francis to hide him from Grandpa.

"And I gave him lots and lots of corn so he wouldn't get hungry," she explained.

Well, even Grandpa had to laugh, finally. And when they went indoors they had to tell it to the others, and they all laughed too.

"It's a wonder Francis didn't raise a fuss, being a prisoner all that time," Jeddie said.

"Well," laughed Grandma, "I think Francis was a stuffed goose —too full of corn to make a fuss!"

By the time they sat down to dinner everyone was in a happy mood.

"I believe I'm going to have a second helping of that turkey," Aunt Cora said as she held out her plate for Father to refill it. "I never realized it before, but I believe I like turkey every bit as well as goose."

Lewis nudged Jeddie, and they smiled secretly at each other as they thought of Francis.

indians for thanksgiving

DOROTHY HEIDERSTADT

It was Thanksgiving Day in New England in 1631. Betsy and her sister Prudence had been left at home while their father and mother went to church. The girls had wanted to go along, but their parents thought the snow was too deep.

60

"Be good," said their father as he shouldered his gun and opened the door. "Keep the fire going and the turkey basting, and keep the doors shut."

The doors had to be kept shut and bolted for the same reason their father had to carry a gun all the time. Indians lurked in the forest—Indians with painted faces, bows and arrows and tomahawks.

Betsy and Prudence had never seen any of the enemy Indians. The only Indians they knew were Red Squirrel and the people of his tribe, who lived back in the forest and were friendly to the white people. But Red Squirrel and the other friendly Indians had moved away almost a year ago, and since then only the white people had lived in the forest.

Betsy and Prudence lived in a log cabin on the edge of the forest. Through the forest ran a path, and at the end of this path, about three miles away, was the church where their father and mother were going.

The two children peered through the window and watched their parents going down the path—their father dressed in his black suit with the wide white collar and the wide white cuffs, with his tall hat on his head, his silver-buckled shoes on his feet, and his long gun on his shoulder; their mother in her gray cloak lined with blue, with the skirt of her long gray dress showing beneath, her little gray cap on her head, and her Bible in her hand. If you have ever seen any pictures of Pilgrims going to Church you will know exactly how Betsy's and Prudence's father and mother looked that day.

Betsy sighed as she watched them go.

"I wish I could have gone along," she said. "Maybe I would have seen an Indian."

"Betsy!" said Prudence in a shocked voice. She frowned sternly at her sister, who was a year younger than she. "You wouldn't want to see an Indian. The only ones you would be likely to see in this forest would be the kind that come with tomahawks!"

"Red Squirrel wasn't that kind," protested Betsy.

"There aren't many Indians like Red Squirrel," said Prudence.

"Come on. I'm going to baste the turkey, and you'll have to help hold the saucepan."

The turkey was roasting on a long pole set across the fireplace, just over the fire. While Betsy held the long-handled saucepan beneath the turkey, Prudence poured spoonfuls of water from the saucepan onto it. This kept the meat from becoming too dry as it roasted.

By and by, when the turkey had been basted enough, Betsy put down the saucepan and went back to the window to look out. The forest lay cold and still in the gray light of the winter morning. The trees were black and bare. The ground was covered with snow, and the snow was covered with little tracks made by rabbits and squirrels. Betsy looked at the forest and went on thinking about Indians.

"Just the same, I would like to see an Indian. Not a big one," she went on hastily. "Just a little one would do. One of Red Squirrel's children."

"Betsy," called Prudence from her chair beside the fire, "what are you talking to yourself about? Come away from that cold window. Let's throw pine cones onto the fire. You like to do that, don't you?"

"Yes," said Betsy reluctantly, moving away from the window. It was fun to throw pine cones onto the fire. They blazed up beautifully. She was quite happy for a while, and she forgot about Red Squirrel's children, whom she missed a great deal. Since they had moved away, she had no other children to play with. Prudence, who was ten, was quite grown up, and liked to bake and knit, and refused to play with dolls any more. The children of the other white people in the forest lived too far away.

Anyhow, nobody, in Betsy's opinion, was as much fun as an Indian child to play with. Indian children knew such lively games and they wore such lovely beads. It was not long before she began to grow tired of the pine cones and to think about Indians again.

Prudence was knitting a muffler for her father. Her knitting needles clicked industriously, and Betsy felt somewhat uneasy as she watched her work. Soon she would have to learn to knit. The

62

thought was almost insufferable. She was sure that she could never learn to do it as it ought to be done.

"Dear me!" said Prudence suddenly, looking at the fire. "We need some more wood. I'll have to go out into the storeroom and get some."

She laid aside her knitting and arose. The storeroom had been built onto the back of the house. In it were piles of wood, pumpkins, potatoes and apples; dried herbs hung down from the ceiling. A door opened into it from the room where the children were.

"Want me to help you?" asked Betsy, jumping up eagerly.

"No," said Prudence. "Stay in here by the fire. You know it's cold out there, and you aren't over your cold yet."

Betsy sighed and wandered over to the window. The morning seemed very long. The good smell of roast turkey filled the room, and her mouth watered. Two hours until dinner time! How could she wait? If she could only have some of it now! If she could only see an Indian!

Suddenly she gasped. Her eyes, which had been wandering aimlessly over the forest, stared at something—something that was moving out there among the trees, something quite small and close to the ground. It looked like a little boy.

"Prudence!" cried Betsy excitedly. "Look! Look! An Indian!"

Prudence dropped her wood with a clatter and flew to the

63

window. "Where? Where?" she gasped, turning pale. Visions of tomahawks and war paint ran through her head.

"There! See?" whispered Betsy, pointing. And just at that moment there emerged from the forest a little Indian boy, all alone. He was about five years old, and he had a little round, fat face and two bright black eyes. He was wrapped in a bright blanket, and he was floundering valiantly through the snow toward the house.

"It must be one of Red Squirrel's children!" cried Prudence. "That means Red Squirrel has come back."

But Betsy was scornful. "Of course, that isn't any of Red Squirrel's children," she announced. "Don't I know exactly what every one of them looks like? This is a strange Indian. Oh, look at him, Prudence! Isn't he cunning?"

The little Indian was standing within a few feet of the door, staring around him curiously and stamping the snow off his moccasined feet.

"Let's get him to come in!" whispered Betsy. "Maybe he's lost. Maybe he's hungry." Her eyes grew large and dark with sympathy at the thought. Was not she herself actually suffering for a taste of that turkey roasting over the fire?

Prudence, meanwhile, had gone to the door and opened it.

"Do come in!" she said politely to the small Indian. "I'm sure you must be cold out there."

"Oh, Prudence!" laughed Betsy, running over to stand beside her. "He doesn't understand what we say."

They flung the door wide open, and beckoned to the little Indian. He looked at them solemnly for a moment. Perhaps he had never before seen two such little girls in long gray dresses, white aprons and buckled shoes. Perhaps he had never seen a house before. At any rate, he remained standing there staring, first at them and then at the house.

Then, just as they were beginning to get cold, and to wonder what to do next, he walked gravely past them into the house. Once there, he continued to look curiously all around him—at the

64

ceiling of the room, at the chairs, the table, the spinning wheel and the fireplace.

At sight of the fireplace, his eyes sparkled. He went close to the fire and held out his hands to it. He sniffed the air hungrily, and Betsy, watching him, felt a pang of hunger too.

"I believe he's hungry," said Prudence. "We must give him something to eat."

"Perhaps we ought to eat with him," suggested Betsy quickly, "so he won't feel impolite to be eating there in front of us."

"And leave Father and Mother to eat their Thanksgiving dinner alone?" demanded Prudence in a shocked voice.

"That's right. We couldn't do it," said Betsy with a sigh.

The table was already set for dinner, although it would still be quite a while before their father and mother would be home.

Prudence and Betsy carved a piece very carefully off the turkey, and put it on a plate. They put a big spoonful of sauce beside it and one of potatoes and gravy. Then they helped the little Indian off with his blanket, and drew up a chair and put him on it in front of the table.

All this time, the little Indian had not said one word. He allowed them to lift him into his chair. But he looked uncertainly at the food on his plate. He picked up the turkey in his hands, hesitantly, and took a bite. Then he laid it down and put out a hand to pick up the potatoes and gravy the same way.

"Wait!" cried Prudence, and he drew back his hand quickly. "He doesn't know how to eat. We'll have to feed him."

So they each got a spoon and took turns feeding the little Indian. First, Prudence would put a spoonful of potatoes and gravy into his mouth. Then when he had swallowed that Betsy would put in a spoonful of sauce. Then the little Indian would take a bite of turkey, and then a bite of bread. They made a game out of it, and presently the little Indian was laughing so much that he could scarcely eat.

Suddenly, in the midst of the game, he looked at the window and gave a pleased, excited cry. He pointed toward the window and

65

began to talk very fast in his own language. He struggled to get down out of his chair.

Betsy and Prudence, somewhat surprised, helped him down and followed him over to the window. He peered out of it eagerly, talking all the while. He kept looking up at them to see whether they understood. He even grew a little impatient with them because they could not understand. They, too, looked out of the window, but there was nothing in sight.

Outside, the snow was falling fast, and so thick were the flakes that the children could see only to the first trees of the forest. All the little rabbit and squirrel tracks were being rapidly filled.

Looking at the little Indian, Prudence wondered uneasily what he had seen through the window. Suppose an Indian had looked in—a wild, savage Indian, the kind who carried a tomahawk! Suppose this was the child of that sort of an Indian! She began to wish that her parents would hurry home.

The little Indian, however, shrugged his shoulders at last and returned to his interrupted meal. When he had eaten everything on his plate, his head suddenly began to nod and he leaned against Prudence's shoulder.

"He's sleepy. Let's carry him over to the old settle by the fire," whispered Prudence. So with much careful tugging and pulling, the two children managed to carry their guest over to the old settle. He slept peacefully. After clearing away his place at the table, Prudence and Betsy returned to the fire, and sat down beside it. Prudence threw some more sticks on it, and then took up her knitting. Betsy, on a low footstool quite close to the old settle, looked at the little Indian.

"Isn't he nice?" she whispered to Prudence. "His tribe must be camping here in the forest, and I suppose he wandered off and got lost. I imagine his mother is worried about him, don't you? He's such a little boy."

"I don't know, I'm sure," said Prudence, counting stitches primly. "I only hope that when they find him here they won't think we were trying to steal him, and tear the house down over our heads."

Betsy put out a hand, and touched the hand of the little Indian. "They won't do that," she said softly. "He will tell them that we are his friends, and that we gave him part of our Thanksgiving dinner."

"I hope so," said Prudence shortly, going on with her stitches.

Betsy leaned drowsily against the settle and looked into the fire. She stiffled a yawn.

"I hope he's going to live here in the forest," she said. "Then we can play with him, and we won't miss Red Squirrel's children so. I've missed them dreadfully."

"And a good thing they went away," said Prudence. "A great girl like you, who should have learned to knit and bake long ago, playing around with Indians!"

But she smiled at her small sister as she said this, and Betsy, who had long since learned that Prudence was not so stern as she sounded, smiled back at her.

"Dear me!" said Prudence suddenly. "I'm a little tired of knitting, myself, right now. I guess everything's ready for dinner. The turkey is in the covered dish close to the fire where it will keep warm. I think I'll rest a while." And she drew her own footstool up close to the settle, and leaned against it as Betsy was doing.

So warm was the room, so drowsy was the sound of the fire purring and crackling on the hearth, that in a few minutes both the children were fast asleep.

This was really too bad, for if Betsy had only remained awake five minutes longer, she would have seen an Indian, such as she had hoped to see if she had gone to church. An Indian was looking in at the window!

Betsy's father and mother, coming down the forest path, were not pleased when they saw several Indians looking in at their front window. In fact, they were badly frightened.

The father shifted his gun under his arm and started forward quickly.

"Wait!" said his wife in a low voice. "Let us see if they are friendly. Speak to them first!"

At the sound of her voice, one of the Indians turned quickly, and

67

the father, much to his relief, recognized the face of Red Squirrel, the friendly Indian, who had moved away.

The other Indians turned around, too. Red Squirrel spoke to them quietly. Then he came forward to greet his friends, the two white people. Silently he made signs for them to come and look in at the window too.

Wondering, they did so. Inside the big room they saw the fire burning on the hearth, the kettle steaming cheerfully, and the table set for Thanksgiving. They saw their children fast asleep beside the settle. They saw the little Indian stretched out comfortably on top of the settle.

One of the strange Indians, who was wearing a large and imposing feather war bonnet, began to talk very fast. He talked for quite a long time, and then stopped suddenly and stood looking at Betsy's and Prudence's father and mother, with snapping black eyes, as though waiting.

"He says," began Red Squirrel, "that he is White Bear, who rules a powerful tribe of the Pequot Indians. This morning the braves in his tribe were to go on the warpath against the white people who live in this forest. As they were leaving, it was discovered that the son of the chief was gone. He had wandered away into the forest. Then this big snow began to fall, and they were afraid that they might not find him again.

"One of them heard the sound of children laughing in this cabin, and looked in at this window. There he saw the chief's son eating at your table. He ran and told the chief.

"Do you understand what your children have done? They have taken in a child of their enemies and warmed him at their fire. He was hungry, and they fed him. He says that he, White Bear, will not forget this. From this day, he will be the friend of the white people of this forest just as I am their friend.

"When I heard that he was coming here to make war on the white people, I came as quickly as I could to see if I could not persuade him to stop. Now it is not necessary. Your children have persuaded him because they have been kind to his son."

When Red Squirrel had finished speaking, the white man held out his hand.

"Come in, all of you," he said, "and share our Thanksgiving dinner."

So the Indians went in, with great dignity, to share the Thanksgiving dinner. Betsy, who was the first of the children to awake, was at first terrified and then delighted when she saw all the Indians. Even Prudence was somewhat thrilled over sitting down to dinner with a real Indian chief who wore such an imposing war-bonnet.

He did not wear the war bonnet during the meal, however. Red Squirrel persuaded him to take it off.

The little Indian boy, whose name, by the way, was Little Wolf, was delighted to see his father. Although he had already been given one Thanksgiving dinner, he found that he was able to eat another.

Poor Betsy, who had been so hungry a little while before, was now so busy staring at the Indians and asking Red Squirrel about his children that she very nearly forgot to eat. After that day, she had a wonderful time with twice as many Indian children to play with as she had had before. She had the children of Red Squirrel's tribe and the children of White Bear's tribe, too. Her mother despaired of ever getting her to learn to bake and knit.

As for the Indians, they were the friends of the white people always, just as they had promised they would be. The powerful tribe of White Bear lived nearby in the forest for many years. In the winter Betsy's and Prudence's mother often found wild game or deer-meat outside her door, left there for her by the Indian hunters. And every Thanksgiving Day, White Bear and Little Wolf and Red Squirrel and several other Indians came to Betsy's and Prudence's house for dinner.

The story of how peace was first made between the tribe of White Bear and the white people in that New England forest became as popular as a fairy tale or a legend. It was told around Indian campfires at night. It was told by white grandmothers to their grandchildren. And from that day on, that peace was kept forever and ever.

thanksgiving on wheels

ELIZABETH HOUGH SECHRIST

The train was so late that Grandpa and Mary Lou had to sit in the station for a long time, waiting. Then when the train was called unexpectedly, they picked up Mary Lou's suitcase and rushed through the gate. Grandpa had just had time to find Mary Lou a seat and talk to the conductor about looking out for her until the train would arrive in Philadelphia. Then the brakeman was shouting, "All aboard," and Mary Lou was waving to Grandpa on the platform. Now the train pulled out of the station, then out of the city. Soon they were moving rapidly past the steel mills and away from Pittsburgh, away from her home and away from her grandparents. The train wheels humming on the tracks seemed to say "away, away, and away."

70

Mary Lou tried not to feel frightened at the thought of the long train ride ahead of her. But she did feel lonely after she had folded her coat and placed it with her hat and mittens on the seat beside her. She thought back over the past few days and all the good-bys she had said. Only yesterday she had bade good-by to her teacher and all her classmates in the sixth grade. She had gone to school up to the last day. Some of her classmates had envied her going to live in Philadelphia. But Mary Lou couldn't imagine how it would be, living anywhere but with Grannie and Grandpa. She thought of how sad Grannie had been to have her go. Aunt Louise had persuaded Mary Lou's grandparents that they were getting too old to keep Mary Lou any longer, that Mary Lou should be with young people more. So here she was, on her way to live with Aunt Louise, Uncle Paul and Betty. Her cousin Betty was only a few months older than Mary Lou, but in many ways she seemed much older. Mary Lou had always stood a little in awe of Betty with her pretty clothes and grown-up manners.

"I don't see why you have to go at all, at all!" Grannie had said that morning as she fried Mary Lou's breakfast egg for the last time.

Mary Lou couldn't remind Grannie that it was because they were getting old, because Grannie would have said "Bosh!" But Mary Lou knew it was true and she noticed, as she watched Grannie packing her lunch, that the old wrinkled hands were shaking worse than usual.

"And I certainly don't understand why you should go off on that long trip on Thanksgiving Day!" she had added indignantly.

"Now Ma, you know why Mary Lou has to go to Philadelphia today," said Grandpa. "Louise said it's the only day Paul can drive into the city from the suburbs to meet her."

And Grannie had replied, "Well, I'm not going to have her ride on that train all day without some good food to eat."

Another thing that made Mary Lou realize that Grannie was getting old was the way she had acted about the five dollars Grandpa had given Mary Lou. Grannie was scared to death somebody on the train would rob Mary Lou. She said she couldn't

71

sleep for thinking how to hide the money on Mary Lou's person so no one would steal it from her. But while she packed Mary Lou's lunch she had an inspiration.

"I know where I can put the money, Mary Lou!" she said. "I'll tie it into your handkerchief and tuck it into the corner of this box, with your lunch."

And that is what she did, with an admonition to Mary Lou to "hang onto your lunch box every minute, Mary Lou, and soon as you get to Aunt Louise's take the money out of the box and put it in a safe place."

And now when Mary Lou recalled Grannie's words about holding on to the box, she came suddenly to a sickening realization. The box! She didn't have it! She tried to think when she had last seen it, and remembered that she had put it on the bench beside her in the station. When she and Grandpa had heard the train being called and had jumped up so quickly, they had left the box on the bench! Mary Lou's heart almost turned over when she thought of losing Grandpa's five dollars. And her lunch! At the thought of the food Grannie had packed for her, tears came to her eyes. "Today's

72

Thanksgiving Day, and I'm not going to let you eat just an ordinary lunch!" Grannie had said. Two fried drumsticks, her favorite part of the chicken! Two cheese and jelly sandwiches and two cinnamon rolls, a banana and a very large piece of chocolate cake with caramel icing that Grannie had baked the day before just for her. And lastly, Grannie had added a package of creamy mints and some shoestring licorice, Mary Lou's favorite candy.

"I have no lunch, and I have no money," Mary Lou said to herself. She still had her railroad ticket and she was clutching it tightly in her hand when the conductor came by.

"I told your granddaddy I'd look after you, Mary Lou," he said kindly. "Are you okay?"

She nodded without speaking, and he punched her ticket and returned it to her. "Just let me know if you want anything," he said absent-mindedly and passed on.

Thinking about her lost lunch made Mary Lou very hungry. She had had her breakfast at five o'clock. She and Grandpa had left on the 6:10 bus in order to get to Pittsburgh in time to make the train. That seemed a long time ago. And her arrival in Philadelphia seemed a long way off. And the wheels kept saying to Mary Lou, "Long, long, long way—"

When Mary Lou wakened it was hard for her to realize, at first, where she was. "I guess I was sleepy, I got up so early," she told herself.

She determined not to think about the lost money and lunch. But when she saw the old lady across the aisle take a package from her bag and start to eat her sandwiches, it made Mary Lou terribly hungry. Just then a man wearing a white jacket came into the car with a huge basket and a large coffee-pot.

"Coffee and sandwiches," he called loudly. "Ham and cheese sandwiches!"

People all up and down the aisle stopped him and bought from him. The man seated in front of Mary Lou ordered a ham sandwich and a cup of coffee. "Fifty cents," the steward said. The old lady across the aisle asked for a cup of coffee. "Fifteen cents," he told her.

73

"Sandwiches? Milk?" he asked, looking straight at Mary Lou. She shook her head and turned to stare out the window. "I wish he'd go away," she thought.

But he didn't. "Traveling all alone?" he asked.

She nodded.

"Dining car's two cars ahead," he told her kindly, and went on to the next passenger.

Soon after, a waiter came through the car calling, "Lunch is being served. Dining-car forward."

Mary Lou wondered what it must be like to eat in a diner. She had seen one from the outside once when a train passed through. She had often thought how grand it would seem to be sitting at a table eating in a restaurant that was speeding through space. Perhaps when she was grown up she would eat in a diner. She began to plan what she would order if that event were ever to happen. And since this was Thanksgiving Day her thoughts turned to turkey. Yes, she would certainly order roast turkey. And filling of course, and mashed potatoes running over with giblet gravy! Then there would have to be cranberry sauce. She wondered if one could order anything one wanted on a train. She thought of her grannie's chocolate cake with caramel icing, and her mouth watered. She was so hungry!

Determined to forget about food, she tried to think of what it would be like living with Aunt Louise and Betty and Uncle Paul. It would be very different, she was sure. And then she thought longingly of her own little room at Grannie's with her single bed and the bureau and the little white chest Grandpa had made for her. She kept all her treasures in her white chest; her dolls and her books and her crayons. She'd left all the dolls behind because she'd been afraid Betty would think her too big to play with dolls. "They'll all be here waiting for you when you come back to visit," Grannie had assured her.

Her thoughts were interrupted when the train came to a stop. When she looked out the window there was no station there, only bleak brown fields and hills dotted here and there with snow. A brakeman walked by, and then another brakeman. The man ahead of her got up presently and walked out of the car. When he came back he spoke to the old lady across the aisle. "There seems to be something wrong farther up the line. The conductor said they would have to wait here for a freight to pass."

"Where are we?" the lady asked.

"Not far from Kittaning, I think."

"Really in the mountains," the old lady replied. The man laughed. "If you can call these mountains," he said. "I'll never forget the time the train I was on was held up by snow in the Rockies. There are your mountains, and that was really snow! We sat there for fourteen hours—nearly froze because the heat went off."

Mary Lou saw to her dismay that it was now snowing hard, and she could picture them being held up for fourteen hours. She wondered what Uncle Paul would do. Would he wait for her or go home without her? And she wondered what time it was. She thought it must be the middle of the afternoon, but presently a waiter came into the car again calling, "Last call to luncheon."

Everyone sat waiting for the train to start again. It was snowing against the pane so thick that Mary Lou could no longer see out. Then the waiter came in again with the basket. This time, besides coffee, he had ice cream and candy. Almost everyone bought hot coffee. The old lady bought some ice cream and ate it very slowly. Mary Lou couldn't keep her eyes off the ice cream until she caught the woman looking at her with an annoyed expression. "I guess she doesn't like me," Mary Lou thought. Then the conductor came through. Several people stopped him with questions about when the train would start. When he came to Mary Lou's seat he stopped. "Are you all right?" he asked.

"Yes," she said faintly. How could she tell him that she was hungry?

He leaned toward her and looked down at her kindly. "We're held up a bit but that freight should be along right soon now."

After he had gone Mary Lou felt more lonely than ever. The snow was piling up fast from what she could see through a small clear space in her window. She thought, maybe they won't be able to get the train started again because there will be so much snow on the tracks. Perhaps she would starve to death. She wondered how long it took to starve. If only she had the five-dollar bill! How awful to be caught on a train in a blizzard with no food and no money. Not a cent! This gave her an idea. She pulled her coat into her lap and started going through her pockets. In one she found a dime! She remembered how Grannie had given it to her for sweeping the porches. In the other pocket she found two pennies. Twelve cents! But what would twelve cents buy? Even coffee was fifteen cents a cup. But somehow she felt better, just knowing that she wasn't penniless. And to her relief the train started up without any trouble after a very long freight train had gone by. It was something to know they were moving at last.

"This train is very late now, isn't it, conductor?" the man in front of her asked when the conductor came through the car again.

"I'm afraid it is, about three hours."

"Can we make it up?" the man asked.

"I'm afraid not too much, with this snow and ice."

Mary Lou wondered again whether Uncle Paul would wait for her.

Several hours passed and she felt weak from hunger. She thought, I *can* wait until I get to Aunt Louise's. Think of all the people on diets; they eat scarcely anything! Then she saw that the waiter had entered the car again with his big basket. "Sandwiches!" he cried. After several stops to sell sandwiches and coffee he stood beside her. He set the basket on the floor, took from it a large paper cup and a bottle of milk.

"How about a nice bottle of milk?" he asked her, removing the cap from the bottle as he spoke. He poured the milk into the cup and handed it to her.

Mary Lou shook her head. "I—I don't believe I want any." When she looked up at him she saw that his black eyes were full of friendliness, and her own eyes filled with tears.

"This one's on me," he smiled. "Besides, I'll bet you're hungry. And every little girl likes milk. I have a little girl just your size. You ought to see *her* drink milk. Her mama says one day she'll turn into a little heifer!"

76

Mary Lou smiled through her tears. She looked at the milk hungrily. Then she put her hand into her pocket and brought out her twelve cents. "Would that pay for it?" she asked.

"Why, honey, that's exactly how much it costs." He took the money and she took the milk.

Mary Lou thought she'd never tasted anything so good in all her life. The milk made her forget the chicken drumsticks and even the five dollars she'd lost, for a moment.

"Tastes pretty good, I guess," said the man.

"I ate my breakfast at five o'clock this morning," Mary Lou told him as she sipped her milk. Then suddenly she was telling him all about losing her lunch box and her money in the box. "I just had twelve cents to my name!" she said, but now Mary Lou was smiling about it as though it were a joke.

Her companion listened sympathetically while Mary Lou told him how it happened that she was riding alone on the train, how she was on her way to live with her Philadelphia relatives.

"That's where I live," he told her, and he assured her that she would like Philadelphia.

"They don't really live *in* Philadelphia," Mary Lou explained. She mentioned the name of the suburb.

"Well, what do you know!" exclaimed the man. "That's where my wife's folks live. Well, it's a small world. My name is James Johnson and hers was Ruby White. Well, what do you know," he laughed, putting the bottle back in the basket. "But now I must get on with my work."

After James had left Mary Lou was amazed at how much better she felt. She didn't feel alone any more. She had made a friend on the train. It was growing dark outside now and the lights had come on in the car. The snow still fell against the window and shut out the rest of the world, making the car seem a little world of its own. The old lady across the way had dropped off to sleep, and Mary Lou's eyes were drooping too. The next thing she knew James was back again, this time without his basket.

"Still here?" he asked, smiling at her.

She nodded and smiled at his joke.

"It won't be long now before dinner will be served up in the dining car. We're serving turkey tonight because it's Thanksgiving." He stopped and looked at her curiously. "Have you ever eaten in a diner?"

He knew she had no money to eat in the diner because she had told him about losing her money. "No," she told him.

"We've got ours all fixed up nice for Thanksgiving," he went on. "Maybe you'd like to see it. If you follow me, I'll show you one of the nicest diners on the line."

Mary Lou hesitated, wondering what Grannie would have wanted her to do. She decided that Grannie would approve of her going to see the diner.

"You'd better put on your coat because it's very cold on the platforms between the cars," he told her.

James helped her into her coat, and then she followed him, waiting while he opened the heavy doors between the cars. She followed him through a parlor car, and then one which he explained was a lounge car. Next they went down a long narrow corridor while the train lurched this way and that, and at last they stepped into the diner. There were the tables just as she had imagined them, all covered with snowy white cloths. To Mary Lou's surprise there were five or six waiters lined up to greet her, all beaming and smiling as if at some secret joke! James led her to a table. It was set for one person. There was a glass of tomato juice in the center of a huge service plate, and a tall glass of milk beside the plate. There were a plate of rolls and a dish of celery and olives on the table. But most surprising of all was the centerpiece! Mary Lou knew at once that it was meant to represent a turkey, though such a queer one she had never seen. Its body and head were fashioned of soft bread, and its wings and funny tail were pieces of leafy celery. It even boasted a red wattle made of pimentos.

Mary Lou sat down in the chair James held for her, feeling a little bewildered. She had no money to pay for a dinner! While the others watched, the head waiter came to her table. "James told us you are riding on the train alone, and that you had lost the lunch your grandmother packed for you," he said politely. "We thought you must be very hungry, so we've fixed up a nice Thanksgiving dinner for you. We'll be mighty pleased to have you be our guest."

Mary Lou was too overwhelmed to think of a reply. And immediately the whole procession of waiters began to serve her. No sooner had she swallowed the last of the tomato juice than a large dinner plate and several side dishes were set before her. Here

was the dinner of her dreams—roast turkey, filling, mashed potatoes smothered in delicious giblet gravy, candied sweet potatoes, creamed onions, lima beans and corn. And the cranberry sauce! It was cut in the form of an apple, with a bit of green gumdrop for a stem, and nestled on crisp lettuce leaves. While she ate, the eager men kept refilling her water glass and milk glass, and offering her more of this and more of that. When she had finished her third piece of turkey and said she could eat no more, they brought her an immense piece of hot mince pie with a generous portion of ice cream on the side. Mary Lou's insides were beginning to feel very full! The last few mouthfuls of pie and ice cream went down very slowly indeed.

Before she had quite finished eating, Mary Lou noticed that the diner was filling up. The waiters were busy now and she watched them as they rushed about between the tables, taking orders, bringing food to the passengers. Mary Lou then began to notice that, every time she looked up, various other occupants of the car were looking and smiling at her. A young woman at the next table leaned toward her and called to her gaily, "Happy Thanksgiving, Mary Lou!" And the gentleman who sat with his back to her, turned in his chair and gave her a broad smile.

"A happy Thanksgiving from me, too, Mary Lou," he said.

Then she knew that the waiters had told the people her name. She felt pleased and happy. She smiled right back at them. "The same to you," she said politely.

When she had finished her dinner she looked around for James. He came and held her coat for her and then accompanied her through the cars to her own seat. As he was turning to leave, she put her hand on his white sleeve and said, "I'll never forget this Thanksgiving Day as long as I live. Never, never!"

It was a tired but happy Mary Lou who got off the train in Philadelphia. The conductor told her to wait until all the passengers had left and he was free to take her to meet her family. But at the last moment James came running up.

"I'm going in to the station to meet my family," he said. "Let *me* take Mary Lou."

He picked up Mary Lou's bag and walked with her to the huge station waiting-room. And there were Aunt Louise and Uncle Paul and Betty waiting for her! And in the excitement of greetings and kisses and explanations, James got away before Mary Lou realized it.

"I'm sorry the train was so late," Mary Lou said.

"Your Uncle Paul called the station before we left home," Aunt Louise explained. "So it was all right. But what a long train ride you must have had!"

"Yes, it was a long ride," Mary Lou said. But, she thought to herself, they would never know how long it seemed!

"Grandpa called up to see if you had arrived safely," Betty told her.

"Yes," said Aunt Louise. "We must call him when we get home and tell him you are with us, all safe and sound! And, Mary Lou, he said to tell you that he and Grannie are coming to spend Christmas with us. We'll see to it that they pay us a nice long visit."

"We always have such fun at Christmas," Betty chimed in.

"And oh, I almost forgot!" Aunt Louise went on to say, "Grandpa found your lunch box right on the bench where you had left it! He said he and Grannie were so worried about you, going all that time without having anything to eat."

"Oh, but I did have something to eat!" And Mary Lou was about to tell them of her surprise Thanksgiving dinner when Betty interrupted.

"You can make up for it when we get home," she said. "Just wait until you see the wonderful Thanksgiving dinner we have waiting at home!"

So Mary Lou didn't have the courage to tell them she had already eaten a Thanksgiving dinner. And it was at that moment that she saw James across the big room, stooping to kiss a little girl just Mary Lou's size. The little girl had flung her arms about her father's neck. She and her mother seemed very happy to see James.

"There's James!" Mary Lou exclaimed.

"Who is James?" asked Uncle Paul.

"Oh, he's a friend I made on the train," she replied as she saw James walk in the other direction with his family. "I guess he's going home to *his* Thanksgiving dinner, too."

As they walked out of the station to the parking lot to get into Uncle Paul's car, Betty squeezed Mary Lou's hand hard.

"I'm so glad you are going to live with us, Mary Lou. I've always wanted a sister. I just know we'll have loads of fun together."

"I know we will, too," said Mary Lou, holding tight, so tight, to Betty's hand. And her heart felt warm and happy.

thanksgiving blues

AILEEN FISHER

Because it was the afternoon before Thanksgiving, Arney didn't have to hand in his arithmetic problems after all. Mrs. Cornwall decided it would be better to have singing for everyone in the room, instead of arithmetic for the only pupil in the fifth grade.

"More like Thanksgiving," she said. "I know Arney has worked his problems, anyway. And this way everybody can join in."

Arney was glad. Not that he felt like singing! He hadn't felt like singing, or whistling either, for four days. And he wasn't sure his arithmetic answers were right.

Usually arithmetic was easy—easy as beating Greta at checkers and Christine at rummy—but this week everything had been hard. Arney couldn't keep his mind off Skipper, couldn't keep the mist from blurring his eyes. Skipper had been the best dog any boy ever had.

They started out singing "Over the River and Through the Woods" because it was the only Thanksgiving song all thirteen pupils knew. Then the first-graders, the Winton twins, wanted to sing it all over again. Arney tried to be a good sport. Yet half the time the words wouldn't come. His mind kept flying off to Skipper, and that did strange things to his throat.

They sang "Oh, Susanna!" and "My Old Kentucky Home," and then Greta asked Mrs. Cornwall if she didn't know another Stephen Foster song she could teach them. Greta always wanted something new. Like begging Mom to put red-checked curtains in the kitchen.

"Why, yes, I know another Stephen Foster song," Mrs. Cornwall said. "It's called 'Jeanie with the Light Brown Hair.'" She

82

hummed the tune for a minute and then she began to sing the words.

"I dream of Jeanie with the light brown hair . . ."

Arney made fists of his cold hands, and blinked. This was almost too much. He wasn't dreaming of Jeanie with the light brown hair, but of Skipper with the black hair and white spots.

When school was over, Arney stayed to help Mrs. Cornwall clean up. He didn't want to walk home with Greta or Christine, or any of the others. They would talk about such silly things. Things that didn't really matter.

"I hope you're going to have a nice Thanksgiving, Arney," Mrs. Cornwall said, as she straightened the things on her desk. She knew about Skipper. Greta had told her the first day after it happened. But she didn't know how much Arney cared. Nobody did.

"I don't think so," Arney said under his breath. Thanksgiving without Skipper, for the first time in ten years! He wanted to change the subject. "Don't you think I'd better empty out the drinking water? If it freezes over Thanksgiving, the pail will bulge all out at the bottom."

He emptied the water, and took out the ashes from the low round stove that stood in the middle of the schoolroom. Then, while Mrs. Cornwall erased the blackboard, he swept out the vestibule. There was an old blue sweater hanging on one of the racks, the hook pok-

83

ing a dent in the back. It had been there as long as Arney could remember. Funny, how a torn old sweater like that could hang around and no one ever want it. While Skipper, who meant so much, was gone and could never come back.

Ahead on the road, Greta and Christine poked along with Ruth and Len Haggard. Behind them, Carl Johnson was just turning off on the side road that led to his house. Arney heard him give a shrill whistle, and pretty soon Carl's big shepherd came bounding up. He jumped around Carl as if he hadn't seen him for a hundred years.

Arney watched. "Well, Shep's all right," he thought. "But he's just a dog. Skipper was like a . . . a *person*. And I won't ever see him again."

No, that wasn't true. Actually, Skipper was everywhere. Arney saw him in all the woods that they had walked through, and under all the bushes where he sniffed for rabbits. Just as plain as day! And his tracks were still pressed into the old snow patch back of the barn.

Arney scuffed down the familiar gravel road that, like everything else, had seemed suddenly strange these past four days. Something was the matter with everything. There was none of that feeling of Thanksgiving that usually came with the end of November. All the places where Skipper had been were so empty they hurt.

The tune of the new song began to run through Arney's head. "I dream of Jeanie with the light brown hair . . ." That was as far as he could go. But it was far enough. The mist was coming in front of his eyes again.

All of a sudden he wanted to catch up with his sisters, wanted to talk and hear someone else talk, wanted to be lifted out of the emptiness he felt. "Wait!" he yelled. "Wait for me."

They turned around and waited. Len had a trick of catching sunlight on his tin lunch pail and shooting it here and there, like a great flashlight. Now he caught a blaze and directed it at Arney, right in his eyes, as he ran ahead. Almost blinded, Arney slowed up. "Hey, Len, put your lunch pail down. I can hardly see." He fumbled for his handkerchief. It was a good excuse to use it, to wipe away that mist before any of them noticed.

As Arney and his sisters said good-by to the Haggards and turned into their lane, and closed the big creaking gate behind them, they could see Dad's truck in the yard.

Arney wondered where Dad had been.

Greta began to hurry ahead. She always wanted to be first to find out about things. "Maybe they forgot something for Thanksgiving when they went to town yesterday. Cranberries, maybe . . ." The words drifted back over her shoulder as her legs began to run.

"Wasn't he going after fence posts today?" Christine asked. She was never in a hurry, like Greta.

Of course, that was it. Arney remembered Dad saying at supper last night that he wanted to drive up to the old Caxton place before it snowed again. He needed some good posts for the winter pasture.

Greta was hopping excitedly around a box on the ground near the truck when Arney and Christine came down the lane. "Just wait till you see," she called. "Just wait till you see."

"What is it?" Arney could see a pile of new split cedar posts near the barn. What else could Greta be talking about?

"Wait till you see! Hurry! Hurry!" she called.

Just then Mom and Dad came out of the kitchen door and started toward the truck.

"Brought you something from Caxton's, son," Dad said, as he met Arney and they crossed the yard together. "She's a little timid. Not used to so much attention. Never had a ride in a truck before, either . . ."

"Hurry and look," Greta urged, bending over the box.

Dad reached down and picked up a little tan-colored dog, half-grown. "She's pretty scared." He put her on the ground and in a flash she turned and hopped back into her box. Everyone laughed, everyone except Arney.

"Isn't she cute!" Greta said. "I'm going to name her Scamper. Did you see how she scampered?"

"She's not yours to name, Greta," Dad said quietly. He turned

85

to Arney. "That's up to Arney. It was tough luck, losing Skipper just before Thanksgiving. I thought you might be glad of another dog. And Caxton thinks this is a good one."

"She's so nice and young," Mom said, "Skipper was getting old. He couldn't have lived *much* longer, anyway."

"I think she's awfully pretty," Christine said.

"Well, what do you think of her?" Dad looked directly at Arney, and so he had to answer.

It wasn't easy. Arney felt his throat swelling again. *Skipper* wasn't ever scared. He never turned tail and tried to hide in a box. He never looked shaky and trembly like that.

"Oh, she's all right, I guess," Arney gulped. He turned toward the house. And then, although he didn't want to, although he tried hard not to, he burst into tears. "But . . . she isn't like Skipper," he sobbed.

They all tried to make him feel better, all at once. Of course she wasn't like Skipper. But she'd learn. Give her a chance. Just wait till she got used to things. Maybe she was a little timid, but she'd get over it. She was smart. And she might even have puppies some day—think of that!

"Well, if you don't want her, son, there's nothing lost," Dad said finally. "If she's going to make you feel worse instead of better, I'll take her back when I go for another load of posts. Old Caxton was going to put her out of the way, anyhow. He sold all the males of the litter, but females . . . well, folks don't go for them so much. Caxton kept this one four months, on the chance that someone would want her."

"Poor little thing, she's scared and strange, that's all," Mom said. "Arney, you take her off alone on a walk and see what you think."

Mom shooed the girls into the house, and Dad started for the barn. He called back kindly. "Remember, there's nothing lost if you don't want her, Arney."

Arney looked down at the box. Timidly the little tan dog looked up. "Well, come on," Arney said.

She didn't budge, only twitched an ear.

"Don't you know how to walk?" Arney demanded.

Two brown eyes stared at him. Then a head ducked down between tan paws.

"You'll always be a *little* dog, won't you? Even when you're full grown. I like *big* dogs. Like Skipper."

There was no sound from the box.

"Well, let's go." Arney picked up the small bundle and set it on the ground. Then he started off toward the river, expecting the dog to follow. But she hopped back in her box again and curled up in the corner.

"What kind of dog are you, anyway?" Arney demanded, coming back and picking her up again. "Well, I'll get you out in the field, away from that box, and then you'll *have* to follow me because there won't be any place else to go."

It was a strange walk. Skipper would have been dashing back and forth, in and out, urging Arney on. Skipper would have caught the scent of a rabbit and galloped through the trees, his tail wagging furiously. Skipper . . .

"Say, didn't you ever take a walk before?" Arney asked. "You keep getting in front of my feet. You keep bumping into me. If you aren't careful, you'll trip me and I'll fall on top of you." Maybe old Caxton thought the dog was smart, but she didn't act it.

They went down to the river, and the place was full of memories. More than almost anywhere else. The little dog kept close to Arney, almost under his feet. He stopped on the bank where the water was swishing around the big rocks.

"Skipper saved my life down here once," he said. "I was just a little kid. I started to wade across, in spring, when the river was swollen. I almost got swept away. But I called Skipper, and he came and let me hang on to him. Skipper was big and strong—not little like *you*."

The little dog was trembling, unused to the sound of water.

Arney leaped out to a big boulder, a few feet from shore. There was a glassy edging of ice around it, above the cold dark water. "Well, come on," he said. "There's plenty of room. Skipper could jump it in his sleep."

On the bank the little dog waited, her tail down, her hind legs shaking.

"Scared?" Arney challenged. "You act like an eggshell, not like a dog. Come on. I'll catch you," he called out crossly.

Two timid brown eyes looked toward the boulder.

"Come on," Arney urged.

With a little whimper the dog crept to the very edge of the bank.

"Come on!"

She tried. But there was a ragged fringe of ice below the bank, and her foot slipped. It all happened so suddenly. Before Arney knew it, she was in the water, swept off her feet.

He leaned over and snatched her up, balancing himself on the rock. She was shivering with cold and fright. Quickly Arney zipped down his jacket and put her inside, next to him, and he could hear her heart thumping against his. "You poor little tike," he said. She was getting his shirt wet, but he didn't mind.

Carefully, he jumped back to the bank and started for home. No, she wasn't like Skipper. But she needed him, just as much as he had once needed Skipper, there in the water. Needed him!

He peeked in at her. She had stopped trembling and was lying quietly in his arms as if she liked it there. Yes, she needed him. There wasn't any doubt about it.

He almost smiled as he looked down at her. "You're sort of pretty," he said. "You've got nice light brown hair." Light brown hair.

Suddenly he heard Mrs. Cornwall singing about Jeanie with the light brown hair.

"Jeanie!" he exclaimed. "Do you know your name's Jeanie?"

A wave of something warm swept over him, and the November air smelled like Thanksgiving, after all.

PLAYS FOR THANKSGIVING

molasses for thanksgiving

JANETTE WOOLSEY

CHARACTERS

THOMAS, *a selectman*

MISTRESS ANNE, *his wife*

FAITH, *his daughter*

NATHAN, *his son*

SAMUEL, *a selectman*

MISTRESS WAITSTILL, *his wife*

PRUDENCE, *his daughter*

MILES, *his son*

CHARITY, *a neighbor's child*

JOSHUA, *a neighbor's child*

ROGER, *a selectman*

JONATHAN, *a townsman*

COTTON, *a townsman*

WILLIAM, *a townsman*

BENJAMIN, *a townsman*

TOWN CRIER

As many other townsmen and children as desired

COSTUMES

MISTRESS ANNE *and* MISTRESS WAITSTILL *wear long black dresses, white kerchiefs, large aprons which tie at the waist and little white caps.* MISTRESS WAITSTILL *also wears a shawl.* LITTLE GIRLS *wear long cotton dresses, aprons and have little black shawls.* BOYS *wear long tight trousers, tucked-in shirts and large collars.* MEN *wear ordinary clothes with leather jackets and broad-brimmed hats.*

91

PROPERTIES

Cupboard. A long table for Act One and a smaller table for Act Two. Candles, cooking utensils, at least four bowls depending on how many children are used for Act Three. A sampler for FAITH, *bell, burlap sack, flour, pumpkin, molasses.*

ACT ONE

TIME: *Early Colonial days.*

PLACE: *Colchester, Connecticut. The scene is the kitchen of* MISTRESS ANNE. *When the curtains open the kitchen is one of great activity.* MISTRESS ANNE *is bustling about setting various ingredients out preparatory to making pies for the Thanksgiving dinner.* FAITH *is tagging after her mother obviously being more trouble than help at this moment.*

MISTRESS ANNE

Faith, how many times have I told you not to follow me about. Have you finished scouring the doorstep as I told you?

FAITH

Yes, I have, Mother. And I swept the floor and I dusted everything.

MISTRESS ANNE

Then work on your sampler. Go over there and sit in the corner out of my way. I declare there is so much work to be done today!
(FAITH *goes over to cupboard, gets her sampler and sits down.*)

FAITH

I can hardly wait. Are we going to celebrate Thanksgiving every year?

MISTRESS ANNE

Indeed, I don't know. The Governor has decreed that everyone in Connecticut celebrate it this week and that's what we're going to do.

FAITH

I think it's exciting. And I'm glad that everyone in the whole town of Colchester is going to have their dinner together, aren't you, Mother?

MISTRESS ANNE

I guess so, I guess so. Faith, go call your brother. I need him now.
(FAITH *jumps up quickly, obviously glad to stop sewing. She runs out.*)

FAITH

Nathan, Nathan come here.
(FAITH *and* NATHAN *run in.*)

NATHAN

Do you want something, Mother?

MISTRESS ANNE

Yes, I want you to get a pumpkin out of the vegetable cellar. And Faith, take a bowl and get some molasses from the molasses cask.

FAITH

(*To* NATHAN.) Pumpkin and molasses! What does that sound like?

NATHAN

(*Clapping his hands.*) Pumpkin pies! Pumpkin pies!

MISTRESS ANNE

(*Sternly.*) Just go right along both of you or there'll be no pies for anyone.
(*She busies herself putting some flour in a bowl as* FAITH *and* NATHAN *run out.* NATHAN *returns quickly, struggling with a huge pumpkin.*)

93

NATHAN

Here it is, Mother. Is this big enough?

MISTRESS ANNE

(*Lifting her hands in disgust.*) Nathan! That's much too large. After all I'm not making all the Thanksgiving pies for the whole town of Colchester.

(FAITH *runs in very much excited.*)

FAITH

Mother, there isn't a drop of molasses!

MISTRESS ANNE

Nonsense! There must be. You're so flighty today, Faith, that you just couldn't see any. My, I'm glad Thanksgiving doesn't come too often. I could never keep you calm if it did. Here, let me have that bowl. I'll get it myself.

(MISTRESS ANNE *leaves.*)

FAITH

Honestly, Nathan, there wasn't a speck. I did look hard.

NATHAN

What'll happen if there isn't any? Maybe we can't have any pies.

FAITH

(*Quickly.*) Oh, no! We just have to have pumpkin pies.

(MISTRESS ANNE *returns looking very much dismayed.*)

MISTRESS ANNE

You're right, Faith. There's no molasses.

(THOMAS *enters with a burlap bag slung over his shoulder. He sets it down.*)

THOMAS

There's the corn. (*He looks at* MISTRESS ANNE *and then at the chil-*

dren.) Well, wife, why such a serious face? Have the children been misbehaving? (*Sternly to* NATHAN.) Speak up, Nathan. What have you been doing to make your mother look like this?

MISTRESS ANNE

(*Quickly.*) Nothing, husband, nothing. The children are not to blame. I was telling them that we have no molasses to make any pumpkin pies.

FAITH

And we need pumpkin pies for Thanksgiving, don't we?

THOMAS

(*Much relieved.*) Can't you borrow some? Surely our neighbors wouldn't mind lending some until the supply ship arrives from New York. It's due any time now. I'll go out now and see if there's been any news.

(THOMAS *leaves.*)

MISTRESS ANNE

Nathan, take the bowl and ask Mistress Waitstill if I may borrow some molasses. Explain we shall return it as soon as we get our next supply.

(NATHAN *goes over to the table to get the bowl and just then there is a knock at the door.* FAITH *opens it and* MILES *comes in. He is carrying a bowl.*)

MILES

Good morning, Mistress Anne. Mistress Waitstill sends her greetings and asks if she may borrow some molasses until the new supply comes in. She has none to make the Thanksgiving pumpkin pies.

MISTRESS ANNE

I'm sorry, Miles. I have none either. I was about to send Nathan over to borrow some from Mistress Waitstill.

95

(*Another knock is heard at the door.* FAITH *opens it and* CHARITY *enters. She is carrying a bowl.*)

CHARITY

Mistress Anne, will you lend my mother some molasses?

MISTRESS ANNE

I would if I could but I haven't any, either. What has happened, anyway? Is everyone out of molasses?

(*Another knock is heard at the door.* NATHAN *opens the door and* JOSHUA *enters. He is carrying a bowl.*)

MISTRESS ANNE

Joshua! Don't tell me! Are you after molasses too?

JOSHUA

Yes, ma'am. We don't have a bit and there are pumpkin pies to be baked. Can we borrow some, please?

MISTRESS ANNE

You could if I had some. But surely there must be some molasses in the town of Colchester.

(*Another knock is heard.* NATHAN *opens the door.* MISTRESS WAITSTILL *enters.*)

MISTRESS WAITSTILL

Good morning, Mistress Anne.

MISTRESS ANNE

Good morning, Mistress Waitstill.

MISTRESS WAITSTILL

I came over to see what is keeping Miles. Miles, you knew I was waiting for you. Why didn't you hurry as I told you?

MILES

Mistress Anne has no molasses.

MISTRESS ANNE

That's right. Not even one drop. And it's beginning to look as though no one else has, either.

MISTRESS WAITSTILL

No molasses? That's ridiculous. Well, we can soon find out. Children, go ask our neighbors. If there isn't any, that means no pumpkin pies for Thanksgiving.

CHILDREN

(*Together in dismay.*) No pumpkin pies?

NATHAN

(*To others.*) Come on. Let's find out.
   (CHILDREN *all leave.*)

MISTRESS ANNE

It is too bad, isn't it? It's such a disappointment. If only Thanksgiving weren't this week.

MISTRESS WAITSTILL

Well, why does it have to be? It could be postponed, couldn't it?

MISTRESS ANNE

(*Slowly.*) I don't know. Maybe it would be breaking the law.

MISTRESS WAITSTILL

There's no law. It's just a proclamation.
   (THOMAS *enters.*)

MISTRESS ANNE

What did you find out?

THOMAS

The ship probably won't be here for another week.

97

MISTRESS WAITSTILL

Couldn't Thanksgiving be postponed? It seems a shame to disappoint everyone. Without pumpkin pies it won't seem right.

THOMAS

(*Amazedly.*) Postpone Thanksgiving?

MISTRESS WAITSTILL

What's wrong with that? The Selectmen could do it, couldn't they?

THOMAS

They could, but would they? That's the question.

MISTRESS WAITSTILL

(*Briskly.*) I know one Selectman who'll vote "Yes." At least he'd better vote that way. And that's my husband, Samuel.

MISTRESS ANNE

Thomas, couldn't you call an emergency town meeting and talk it over?

THOMAS

I'll talk to Roger and Samuel. They're the other Selectmen. Now no promises, mind you, but we'll see.
(THOMAS *leaves.*)

MISTRESS WAITSTILL

I'd better go and see Samuel first. Then I'll be sure.

MISTRESS ANNE

Does Samuel always do as you want him to?

MISTRESS WAITSTILL

(*Emphatically.*) Almost always!
(MISTRESS WAITSTILL *leaves.* MISTRESS ANNE *is putting away the flour as* FAITH *and* NATHAN *burst in.*)

98

MISTRESS ANNE

(*Sharply.*) Not so fast. Your manners are most unseemly today. (*Both children calm down.*) And now can you tell me what you found out?

FAITH

It's true, Mother. There's not a drop of molasses in the whole town of Colchester.

NATHAN

How will you make the pies, Mother?

MISTRESS ANNE

There'll be no pies—unless—Thanksgiving is postponed.

NATHAN and FAITH

(*Together.*) Postponed?

MISTRESS ANNE

(*Nodding her head.*) Yes, that's what I mean. Thanksgiving may be postponed.

(*curtain*)

(*Between Act One and Act Two the* TOWN CRIER, *ringing bell, walks slowly back and forth in front of the closed curtain.*)

TOWN CRIER

Hear ye! Hear ye! Town meeting at eight o'clock tomorrow morning! Hear ye! Hear ye! Town meeting at eight o'clock tomorrow morning!

ACT TWO

TIME: *The next morning.*

PLACE: *Town Hall. Benches or chairs are arranged facing a table at which* THOMAS, ROGER *and* SAMUEL *are sitting. As the other men come in they seat themselves quietly and just say a word or two in greeting to their neighbors. They keep their hats on except when they get up to speak. Then the speaker takes his off, but puts it on again as soon as he is finished. Everything is very solemn. Town Meetings were not called very often and this is a serious affair. When everyone is in his seat* ROGER *speaks.*

ROGER

(*Standing.*) Fellow citizens of the town of Colchester. Your Selectmen have called you together to discuss what seems to be a serious subject. As you all know we have been chosen by you to run the town and we usually make the decisions ourselves. But this problem seems to be of such a nature that we feel you should have a voice in helping to decide what to do. I shall let Thomas explain it to you.

(*As* ROGER *sits down,* THOMAS *stands. He is embarrassed and he hesitates as he tries to begin.*)

THOMAS

We-ll, you see—I guess maybe you already know—the fact is, there's no molasses and our womenfolk are mighty upset. (*There is a little murmur in the audience as the different men nod their heads and comment to their neighbors. Apparently they all know the situation.* ROGER *raps for order and* THOMAS *continues.*) Now it seems as though our womenfolk think that Thanksgiving is not the same without pumpkin pies and they say they can't make a proper pie without molasses! (*Another murmur goes through the crowd as they discuss this apparent emergency with their neighbors.*) The point seems to be, what are we going to do about it?

100

(THOMAS *sits down abruptly.*)

ROGER

Samuel, you have a suggestion. Suppose you tell us what it is.

SAMUEL

(*Arising.*) I propose we postpone Thanksgiving until the supply ship comes in.

(*He sits down and this time there is more than a murmur. Several men want recognition.* ROGER *raps for order again.*)

ROGER

Jonathan, what's on your mind?

JONATHAN

(*Getting up and removing his hat.*) Just this. Who do we think we are, to go against the Governor's proclamation? He set Thanksgiving for this week, didn't he? Not next week, nor the week after nor the week after that. This week was when he set Thanksgiving and I think it ought to stay that way.

(*He sits down and claps his hat on his head emphatically.*)

ROGER

Cotton, you're next. Speak up.

COTTON

(*Arising with dignity and removing his hat with a sweeping gesture.*) We're the town of Colchester! And we're proud of it! And if we want Thanksgiving in the middle of the summer we've got every right to have it then!

(*There are many murmurs of assent as* COTTON *sits down.*)

ROGER

All right, William, speak your piece too.

WILLIAM

It's easy to see that Samuel has been influenced by his good wife,

101

Mistress Waitstill. It is well known that Mistress Waitstill is a strong-minded woman.

(*There are cries of "Shame, shame" as* WILLIAM *sits down again.* ROGER *raps for order.*)

ROGER

(*Mildly.*) Perhaps William will feel differently after he is married a longer time. But this is no time for personal remarks. If anyone has anything more to say, let him be heard before we vote on what we're going to do. Benjamin, what is your opinion?

(BENJAMIN *is old and leans heavily on a cane. He speaks in a quavery voice.*)

BENJAMIN

I say, let the women have their way, bless them! And let them have pumpkin pies for Thanksgiving if they want them.

(*There are many nods of agreement as* BENJAMIN *sits down.* COTTON *is trying to get* ROGER'S *attention.*)

ROGER

Cotton?

COTTON

How do you Selectmen feel? After all, you were elected because we have faith in your good judgment. What are your ideas on the subject, Roger?

ROGER

Well, we feel that Thanksgiving should be a happy time. The first Thanksgiving was celebrated because everyone was grateful for the bounteous harvest and there was rejoicing. Now we feel that everyone will be in a more cheerful frame of mind if we wait until that ship comes in. Surely it's not going to make any difference to the Governor if we give thanks next week instead of this week. Jonathan?

102

JONATHAN

Before we decide to do anything about it, hadn't we better consult the Governor?

ROGER

I don't think that's necessary. No law has been passed so we're not breaking any.

JONATHAN

I, for one, don't want to offend the Governor by setting aside his proclamation. But if everyone else decides to vote "yes" I'll vote that way too.

(WILLIAM *asks for recognition.*)

ROGER

William, we'll hear from you.

WILLIAM

I apologize to Mistress Waitstill and I just want to say 'twill be a pleasure to eat one of her pumpkin pies.

ROGER

Are there any more opinions to be offered? No? Then we will vote. Thomas, put your idea in the form of a motion, please.

THOMAS

I move that we postpone Thanksgiving until two days after the supply ship comes in.

SAMUEL

And I second it.

ROGER

You have heard the motion. All those in favor say "Aye."

ALL

Aye.

ROGER

Opposed. "No." (*There are no "No's"*) The Ayes have it and Thanksgiving is postponed.

(*curtain*)

ACT THREE

TIME: *The day after the supply ship's arrival.*
PLACE: *Same as Act One, the kitchen of* MISTRESS ANNE. MISTRESS ANNE *is bustling around and, as usual,* FAITH *is getting in her way.*

MISTRESS ANNE

Faith, you will have to calm yourself. Get your sampler and sit down as a well-brought-up child should. I'm sure no other little girl acts as you do.

FAITH

(*Getting her sampler and sitting down.*) I'm sorry, Mother, I truly am. But I'm excited although I really try not to be. Oh, Mother, aren't you glad that tomorrow is Thanksgiving?

104

MISTRESS ANNE

All I can say is that I hope that this time we have it and that nothing more goes wrong. It is time for your father and Nathan to be back. They've been gone for hours. Surely it hasn't taken them all this time to get our supplies from the ship.

FAITH

Um-um. I can just taste those pumpkin pies. I've missed not having molasses, haven't you, Mother? And can I have some on a piece of bread when they get here?

MISTRESS ANNE

Child, child, how your tongue does run on! Don't you know that good children should be seen and not heard?

FAITH

(*Contritely.*) I'm sorry, Mother. I'm always forgetting. But somehow I can't seem to help it today.

(*Just then* NATHAN *rushes in. He is very excited and all out of breath.*)

NATHAN

Mother, Mother!

(FAITH *jumps off her chair and her sampler falls to the floor.*)

MISTRESS ANNE

Now, Nathan, not so fast, please. Faith, pick up your sampler immediately and sit down.

(FAITH *picks her sampler up and does as her mother tells her, but she does it reluctantly.*)

FAITH

Yes, Mother.

MISTRESS ANNE

Now, Nathan, a little more slowly. Where is your father?

NATHAN

He's coming as soon as he takes care of the horses.

MISTRESS ANNE

And why aren't you helping him?

NATHAN

I will, Mother. (*He starts toward the door and says over his shoulder.*) I thought you'd want to know that we lost the molasses.

(FAITH *jumps up and once more her sampler falls to the floor. This time* MISTRESS ANNE *pays no attention to* FAITH.)

MISTRESS ANNE

What did you say, Nathan? Come back in here at once, young man.

NATHAN

(*Meekly.*) Yes, ma'am.

(THOMAS *enters and* MISTRESS ANNE *turns to him.*)

MISTRESS ANNE

What did Nathan mean? Did you really lose our molasses? What happened?

FAITH

(*Beginning to cry.*) Does that mean we can't have any pumpkin pies for Thanksgiving?

MISTRESS ANNE

Faith, hush this very instant. Thomas, tell me quickly. What happened?

THOMAS

When we were coming up the hill just outside of town the cask got loose from the rope and before I knew what had happened it rolled off the back of the wagon. Down the hill it went and hit a rock alongside the road and smashed to pieces!

106

MISTRESS ANNE

Oh, oh, oh! How dreadful!

NATHAN

And Mother, you should see that molasses! It's all over everything.
(*A knock is heard at the door.*)

MISTRESS ANNE

Go see who it is, Faith.
(FAITH *goes to the door wiping her eyes with the corner of her apron.* MISTRESS WAITSTILL *enters with a bowl of molasses.*)

MISTRESS WAITSTILL

I heard you had some bad luck today. Here's some of my molasses.
Use this until you get some more.

MISTRESS ANNE

Oh, you're so kind. Thank you very much, Mistress Waitstill.
(MISTRESS ANNE *takes bowl and sets it on the table.*)

MISTRESS WAITSTILL

I hear that Jonathan is having quite a time. His hogs found your molasses and I guess they thought it was mud. Anyway they've been rolling in it and they're a sight, I can tell you.
(FAITH *and* NATHAN *begin to laugh behind their hands.*)

MISTRESS ANNE

(*Sharply.*) Stop that, both of you! It isn't kind to laugh at another's misfortunes.

MISTRESS WAITSTILL

If he kept his hogs penned up as he should it wouldn't have happened.

THOMAS

He'll probably have a lot to say about this. He didn't want Thanksgiving postponed in the first place.

107

(*Another knock is heard at the door and as* FAITH *opens it* CHARITY *comes in. She is carrying a bowl of molasses.*)

CHARITY

Mother just heard about your molasses being spilled so she sent this bowlful over to you.

(MISTRESS ANNE *takes it and sets it on the table.*)

MISTRESS ANNE

Thank you, Charity, and tell your mother I'm grateful. With yours and Mistress Waitstill's, we can have some pies too.

CHARITY

I'll tell her, ma'am. And now I must go. I have to help tend the little children so they will be out of Mother's way.

(CHARITY *leaves and is almost knocked down by* MILES *and* PRUDENCE *as they rush in.*)

MISTRESS WAITSTILL

(*Sharply.*) Prudence! Miles! Have you no respect for Mistress Anne that you rush into her house without asking permission?

(PRUDENCE *is crying. Her face, hands and clothes are covered with molasses.* MILES *looks no better.* PRUDENCE *rushes to her mother and grabs hold of her apron.*)

PRUDENCE

Mother, Mother! Make Miles stop. He's been putting molasses all over me.

MILES

Prudence started it, Mother, honestly she did. She put it on me first.

(MISTRESS WAITSTILL *takes each one by the ear and grimly marches them to the door. Both children begin to howl loudly.*)

108

MISTRESS WAITSTILL

Home you go! Neither one of you deserves a bit of Thanksgiving turkey! The idea of fighting with molasses!

(MISTRESS WAITSTILL, PRUDENCE *and* MILES *leave. As they go there is a procession of children coming in each bearing a bowl of molasses. They are saying, "Mother sent this." "Mother wants you to have some of our molasses."* MISTRESS ANNE *thanks each one and puts the bowls on the table. When the last child has gone* MISTRESS ANNE, THOMAS, FAITH *and* NATHAN *gather around the table and look at all the bowls. Suddenly they all laugh.*)

MISTRESS ANNE

Thomas, I guess I'll have to forgive you. But right now I'm thinking how thankful we should be that we have such wonderful friends and neighbors.

THOMAS

And I promise you that the next cask of molasses I get I'll tie on the wagon so tightly it'll *never* roll off.

(FAITH *and* NATHAN *take hands and jump around.*)

FAITH and NATHAN

Molasses for pumpkin pies! Pumpkin pies for Thanksgiving!

MISTRESS ANNE

Children! Children!

(*But the children continue dancing and singing.*)

(*curtain*)

a quiet thanksgiving

JANETTE WOOLSEY

CHARACTERS

GRANDMA JOHNSON
DAN JOHNSON, *her son*
MARY JOHNSON, *his wife*
GEORGE ⎫
RUTH ⎭ *their children*
MRS. MABEL MASON, *Grandma's daughter*
LYNN MASON, *her husband*

JENNY ⎫
PAUL ⎭ *their children*
SAM WILLIS, *a neighbor*
SALLY ⎫
JIMMY ⎭ *his children*
MR. TIMSON, *a peddler*
MR. COLLINGWOOD
MRS. COLLINGWOOD
ROGER, *their son*

COSTUMES

GRANDMA *and* MARY *wear gingham dresses which come almost to the floor and large aprons which tie around the waist.* GRANDMA'S *gray hair is pulled back tightly into a knot at the back of her head.* MARY'S, *in an attempt to be more fashionable, is worn on top. Hair styles in 1912 were topheavy and often a circular pad was worn and the hair arranged over it.* MABEL *wears a shirt-waist and a long skirt. When she first comes in she has on a long coat.*

110

Her hat has a large crown and brim and is trimmed with velvet or taffeta bows. MRS. COLLINGWOOD *is very elaborately dressed. She wears a suit which has a long and very tight skirt. It may be slit up the side a bit. This was the era of hobble skirts and fashionable women always wore them for street wear. Over this suit she wears a linen or pongee duster. Her hat may be elaborate, trimmed with feathers or flowers (flowers were worn in the winter too) or it may be less elaborate and worn with a large veil which ties under the chin. She carries a large muff and wears a great deal of jewelry.*

DAN JOHNSON, LYNN MASON *and* SAM WILLIS *wear ordinary clothes.* LYNN *wears a derby but* DAN *and* SAM *wear caps with flaps which cover their ears.* MR. COLLINGWOOD *wears a motor costume which consists of a long duster, a fancy cap and goggles.* MR. TIMSON *has on a suit which looks a little the worse for wear. He has no overcoat and his coat is pinned together at the neck with a safety pin. His derby hat is pretty well battered.*

RUTH, JENNY *and* SALLY *wear woolen dresses which come well below the knees. Over the dresses they wear pinafores. Of course they wear long black stockings. For outdoors they wear ordinary coats and stocking caps which have long tassels.*

GEORGE, PAUL, JIMMY *and* ROGER *wear ordinary clothes except that the trousers must be short. They, too, with the exception of* ROGER *wear stocking caps. He wears a hat with a turned up brim.*

PROPERTIES

The scene is laid in a dining room which is also used as a living room. A dining room table which can be extended by adding leaves is needed; a couch; at least one or two old fashioned rocking-chairs; a number of straight chairs, dishes, silverware and anything else which can be used on the table. MR. TIMSON'S *pack should be made of black oilcloth. It is knotted in such a manner that a stick can be slipped through so that he can carry it over his shoulder. A folded shawl lies over the back of a chair.*

111

IT'S TIME FOR THANKSGIVING

PRODUCTION NOTE

Costumes are an important part of this play and can make it very amusing. An attempt should be made in so far as possible to duplicate the styles of 1912.

TIME: *Thanksgiving Day, 1912.*

PLACE: *The living room of a farmhouse.*

(*When the curtain opens* MARY *and* GRANDMA JOHNSON *are setting the table.*)

GRANDMA

It won't seem like Thanksgiving this year with just the five of us to eat that big turkey. It'll be too quiet with no company, and I don't like it.

MARY

You're right, Mother Johnson. And why Dan had to save that big gobbler for us I'll never know. It must weigh twenty pounds if it weighs an ounce. We'll be eating it until Christmas and then it'll be time to have another.

GRANDMA

I remember when this house was full to overflowing with people at Thanksgiving. Of course that was when all my children were younger. Now here it is 1912 and they're all married and have families of their own. They don't care about making the trip home any more.

MARY

Now, Mother Johnson, you mustn't talk like that. You know they'll all be here for Christmas as usual. It's just that it's hard to make two trips so close together.

112

GRANDMA

I'm sorry, Mary. I know I shouldn't complain. I'm thankful that Dan decided to come back home and take over the farm after his father died. It would be pretty lonesome for me if it weren't for you and the children to keep me company.

MARY

We've loved it. I never thought Dan was happy in the city. And the children are better off here, too. This country life has been good for them. By the way, where are Ruth and George? Have you seen them?

GRANDMA

I saw them go out to the barn with their father a few minutes ago. He told them that the tiger cat, Goblin, as the children call her, has six new kittens. (*Disgustedly.*) Goblin! Such a heathenish name, even for a cat!

MARY

Don't you think she looks sort of spooky with that black stripe under each eye? I think the children chose a good name. But six more cats! The children will never want to part with any of them. We'll simply have to find homes for them or one of these days we'll have to move out and let the cats take over!

(*The door bursts open and* RUTH *rushes in.*)

RUTH

(*Excitedly.*) Mother! Grandma! Guess what! There's a team coming up the lane and it's bringing Aunt Mabel, Uncle Lynn, Jenny and Paul.

GRANDMA

Where's my shawl? (*Looking around and then seeing it on the chair.*) Oh, here it is.

(GRANDMA *snatches up her shawl, throws it around her and leaves hastily.* MARY *goes over to the door and stands there a minute.*)

113

MARY

(*Calling out.*) Happy Thanksgiving, everyone! Come on in. You'll freeze standing out there.

(GRANDMA, MABEL, RUTH, GEORGE, JENNY *and* PAUL *come in.* MARY *kisses* MABEL.)

MARY

(*Looking out the door.*) Where are the men?

MABEL

Talking to the driver from the livery stable I guess.

GRANDMA

Now this is what I call a nice surprise. When did you decide to come?

MABEL

I woke up early this morning and I got to thinking how nice it would be to have Thanksgiving with you, Mother. So I woke up Lynn and said, "If we hurry we can catch the milk train and have Thanksgiving with Mother."

MARY

I'm certainly glad you're here. Mother Johnson and I were just complaining that we had too much turkey.

GRANDMA

Dan was pretty smart after all, wasn't he? He must have had a feeling that we'd need a big one. (*Hugging* JENNY.) I was dreading a real quiet Thanksgiving.

MARY

(*To* MABEL.) Go right upstairs and take off your things. You can put them in the spare room.

114

MABEL

Come on, children.

RUTH

I want to show Jenny our new kittens.

PAUL

(*To* GEORGE.) Grandma wrote that Uncle Dan had gotten you a new pony.

GEORGE

He's a dandy. Wait until you see him.

GRANDMA

(*Shooing with her apron.*) Then out you go! You children clear out from underfoot. We've plenty to do now.
   (*The children go out as* DAN *and* LYNN *enter.*)

MARY

(*Shaking hands with* LYNN.) It's good to see you, Lynn.

LYNN

And it's good to be here. I had a feeling that Thanksgiving was going to be rather unhappy at our house. But Mabel had decided that we shouldn't make two trips this year so I left it up to her. To tell the truth I wasn't surprised when she changed her mind this morning.

DAN

How is that team you hired from the livery? I heard in town that Tom White had added a couple of new horses to his stable but I hadn't seen them until you drove up today.

115

LYNN

They look like good ones to me. They certainly step right along. It took us only about half an hour to come out here from the station.

GRANDMA

Mary, we'd better put another leaf in the table.

(MARY *goes out to get the leaf and* GRANDMA *begins to clear the table.*)

DAN

(*To* LYNN.) Like to walk about the farm a little before you take off your things?

LYNN

I wouldn't mind a little exercise. (*To* GRANDMA.) Will you have enough food if I work up an appetite, Mother Johnson?

GRANDMA

Oh, go along with you! Have you ever been hungry in my house yet?

LYNN

(*Emphatically.*) Never!

(DAN *and* LYNN *leave.* MABEL *comes in from one side as* MARY *carrying the table leaf enters from the other.*)

MABEL

Here, let me help do that.

(MABEL *takes leaf from* MARY *and she and* GRANDMA *put it in the table.*)

MARY

I'll go out and peel some more potatoes.

(MARY *leaves and* GRANDMA *and* MABEL *start resetting the table.*)

116

MABEL

Guess who we saw walking along the road as we were driving from the station—old Mr. Timson, the peddler. We asked him to get in and ride with us but he wouldn't do it.

GRANDMA

(*Calling to* MARY.) Better peel a few more, Mary. Mr. Timson is on his way. (*To* MABEL.) No, he never rides with anyone. He always walks.

MABEL

I'd almost forgotten Mr. Timson. My goodness, I wonder how old he is. I remember him coming here when I was a little girl.

GRANDMA

He's getting along. But he still keeps on coming. I'm surprised he's around at this time of the year, though. Usually he goes through here earlier in the fall on his way south. Maybe he's been sick.

MABEL

I wouldn't mind getting a few things myself. I've been intending to get some lace for some petticoats I'm making for Jenny and I need some buttons too.

GRANDMA

I thought he'd skipped us this year. I always buy my calico for my aprons from him.

MABEL

Does he still carry the tin box with all the jewelry? How that always fascinated me!

GRANDMA

Yes, he does. And probably you'll recognize some of it too. I'm sure he's been carrying some of that jewelry for years.

117

MABEL

He always used to get here just at meal time.

GRANDMA

He still does. He hasn't missed dinner with us for years. He's always welcome too.
(*A knock is heard at the door.*)

MABEL

That must be Mr. Timson now.
(GRANDMA *goes to the door.*)

GRANDMA

How do you do, Mr. Timson? Come right in.
(MR. TIMSON *enters. He looks old and is very stooped. He carries his oilcloth pack on a stick over his shoulder.*)

MR. TIMSON

Howdy, Mrs. Johnson. Would you like anything today?

GRANDMA

Well now, Mr. Timson, we're pretty busy getting ready for our Thanksgiving dinner. But we'd be pleased to have you stay and eat with us and we'll look at your things afterward.

MR. TIMSON

That's right kind of you ma'am. Are you sure I won't be in the way?

GRANDMA

(*Briskly.*) Of course I'm sure. We're always glad to have you. But aren't you a little late this year?

MR. TIMSON

Yes, ma'am. I am. I've had a sick spell but I'm better now.

GRANDMA

That's good. This is my daughter, Mr. Timson. Maybe you remember Mabel. She's my youngest. She's Mrs. Mason now.

MABEL

I remember you, Mr. Timson, whether you remember me or not.

MR. TIMSON

I guess I wouldn't have known you. You've changed since I last saw you. All grown up now, aren't you?

MABEL

All grown up is right and with two youngsters of my own. You look tired. Why don't you sit down and make yourself comfortable until dinner time?

MR. TIMSON

Now I wouldn't mind that at all. I get a bit tuckered out these days. Can't understand why. I never did before.

(MR. TIMSON *puts his pack on the floor beside the chair. He takes off his battered hat and brushes it carefully with his sleeve and then places it on top of his pack. He lowers himself slowly into the chair, puts his head back and falls asleep almost immediately.* GRANDMA *looks at him, shakes her head and murmurs "Poor soul" sympathetically.* MABEL *goes over to the window and looks out.*)

MABEL

I believe you're about to get more company, Mother. It looks like Sam Willis.

(GRANDMA *goes over to the window.*)

GRANDMA

That's just who it is. He and his wife, Sarah, are good friends of Mary and Dan. (*Calling.*) Mary, you're getting company.

(MARY *enters wiping her hands on a towel.*)

119

MARY

Who is it?

GRANDMA

It's Sam Willis.
(MARY *opens door.*)

MARY

Come in, Sam. Happy Thanksgiving to you.

SAM

Thanks, Mary. Good morning, Mrs. Johnson. (*Noticing* MABEL.) And Mabel! This is a surprise! (*Shaking hands with* MABEL.)

MABEL

Hello, Sam. It's nice to see you again. How's Sarah?

SAM

Sarah's all right but her sister isn't and that's what I stopped in about. Last night we got word that she had fallen and broken her ankle. Sarah feels that she should go over and help out and we were wondering if you could take Sally and Jimmy for a few days.

MARY

Of course we'd be glad to. Ruth and George will be tickled pink.

SAM

We thought you'd say that. In fact we counted on it. The children are with us and I'll just get them and their suitcase.

GRANDMA

Won't you and Sarah come in and have dinner with us before you go?

SAM

No thanks, Mrs. Johnson. It's quite a drive over to Martha's and we must be on our way.

120

MARY

Tell Sally and Jimmy that the other youngsters are playing in the barn and to run on out there. Sarah is not to worry about them. They'll get along just fine. Give my love to Martha and tell her we're sorry.

SAM

Thanks a lot, Mary. I'll bring the bag right in.

(SAM *leaves to get the bag and* GRANDMA *begins to count the places at the table.*)

GRANDMA

Let's see, three more makes twelve. Guess we need another leaf. Come on, Mabel, give me a hand.

MARY

(*Laughing.*) You love this, don't you, Mother Johnson?

GRANDMA

It's beginning to seem more like Thanksgiving every minute.

(GRANDMA *and* MABEL *begin to clear the table.* MARY *goes out and brings in another leaf which she stands up against the wall. Then she opens the door and takes a suitcase from* SAM.)

MARY

Good-by, Sam.

SAM

Good-by, and thanks again.

(MARY *goes into the kitchen and* GRANDMA *and* MABEL *finish clearing the table, put the extra leaf in and begin to set the table again. As they work they continue their conversation.*)

MABEL

This table can certainly grow, can't it Mother?

GRANDMA

It can grow more than this too. When you and all the other children come home with your families it will really stretch.

MABEL

Will everyone be home for Christmas this year?

GRANDMA

I've heard from everyone except Jerry. But you know him. He'll probably put off writing until so late that he'll have to carry the letter himself!

MABEL

Well, this is finished once more. I'm going to see if I can help Mary.

(GRANDMA *and* MABEL *leave for the kitchen as* DAN *and* LYNN *enter from outdoors.*)

LYNN

How was your apple crop this year, Dan?

DAN

It looked good to me, and Mother said it was the best in years. (*Sees* MR. TIMSON.) We-ll! It looks as though we have another guest.

LYNN

Who is it?

DAN

Mr. Timson. Ever since I can remember he's been coming through here once a year with his pack. And he always arrives just before dinner. I've often wondered how he manages to time himself so well.

LYNN

Perhaps we shouldn't talk so loudly. We may wake him up.

122

DAN

No chance. He always takes a little nap before dinner and mere words never disturb him. We actually have to shake him to arouse him.

LYNN

(*Looking at table.*) That table looks some larger than it did. You must have gotten some unexpected company.

DAN

Most welcome company, I assure you.

(*Suddenly a very loud noise is heard outside. It sounds like a gun going off.* LYNN *and* DAN *jump to their feet and rush to the window.* MR. TIMSON *wakes up and sits up looking all around. Satisfied that nothing is happening to him he settles down and goes back to sleep.* GRANDMA, MABEL *and* MARY *rush in from the kitchen.*)

MABEL

What in the world was that?

GRANDMA

Land sakes! Who's shooting off firecrackers on Thanksgiving?

LYNN

No one, Mother Johnson. But just look out here.

(GRANDMA, MABEL *and* MARY *crowd in around the window.*)

MARY

Why it's an automobile. What happened?

DAN

A tire blew out.

GRANDMA

I never saw an automobile like that before. Look. The back seat is all enclosed with glass.

123

LYNN

It's called a limousine and that is a Packard. I heard that it costs around six thousand five hundred dollars.

DAN

Whew! It takes a rich man to own one of those.

MABEL

The children are fascinated. Look at them all standing around with their mouths open.

GRANDMA

Rich or no rich, those people must be cold. Dan, ask them to come in where it's warm until the tire is fixed. That man seems to be having a hard time.

DAN

That man, as you call him Mother, is a chauffeur.
(DAN *goes out doors.*)

MABEL

(*Sighing.*) Some day I'd like to have an automobile and wear clothes like that.

GRANDMA

You couldn't get me in one of those new fangled contraptions for anything. I'll stick to the horse and buggy.

MARY

Here they come.
(*The door opens and a very stylishly-dressed woman, her husband and their little boy enter with* DAN. *The woman walks with little mincing steps and indeed she can do nothing else because she is wearing a hobble skirt.*)

124

DAN

This is Mr. and Mrs. Collingwood and their son, Roger. And this is my mother, my wife, my sister, Mrs. Mason and her husband.

MARY

Won't you sit down?

MRS. COLLINGWOOD

Thank you.

(*Everyone sits with the exception of* ROGER. *He walks around looking at everything.*)

ROGER

(*Whining.*) When are we going to go on? I want to go. (*Pointing at* MR. TIMSON.) Who is that?

MARY

That's Mr. Timson, a guest. He's walked a long way and he's tired.

MRS. COLLINGWOOD

We're sorry to impose on you like this. How long will it take Adams to fix the tire, Allan?

MR. COLLINGWOOD

I'm not sure. This is the first time this has happened to us. You see we are looking for a place to have our dinner. We had intended to stop at the hotel in the town we just came through but it was closed.

GRANDMA

Of course it's closed. It's an outlandish custom to eat in a hotel on Thanksgiving Day.

MABEL

Now, Mother!

MR. COLLINGWOOD

No doubt you are right, Mrs. Johnson, but I'd heard that the meals were excellent and that people come from a distance to eat there.

125

MARY

That's true. It's quite famous for its fine food. But it's always closed on Thanksgiving and Christmas.

GRANDMA

And you won't find another hotel for miles even if you do get that automobile of yours going again.

MRS. COLLINGWOOD

What shall we do, Allan? You know I was against this idea of driving somewhere right from the beginning.

MR. COLLINGWOOD

But it was your plan to let the cook and the maid have a holiday, remember?

ROGER

(*Whining.*) I want to get started.

MRS. COLLINGWOOD

(*Sternly.*) Roger, sit down and be quiet.

MARY

Roger, why don't you go out and play with the children? I'm sure they'd be glad to have you.

ROGER

I don't want to.

MR. COLLINGWOOD

Yes, go on out, Roger. It'll make the time go faster.

ROGER

Oh, all right.
   (ROGER *leaves. A silence falls on the group.*)

126

GRANDMA

(*Suddenly.*) Now why don't you folks stay and have dinner with us? I reckon we can give you as good a meal as you would have had at the Washington House.

(MARY *looks startled but she quickly seconds the invitation.*)

MARY

Please do. We'd be happy to have you.

MR. COLLINGWOOD

Thank you but we couldn't possibly accept. It's too much of an imposition.

(*Ruth rushes in.*)

RUTH

(*Screaming.*) Mamma, Papa! The little boy fell through the ice. We told him not to go on the pond but he went anyway.

(MR. COLLINGWOOD, DAN, LYNN *and* RUTH *rush out.* MRS. COLLINGWOOD *starts for the door as fast as she is able.*)

MRS. COLLINGWOOD

Oh, my poor Roger. Will he drown?

GRANDMA

Not a chance. It's not that deep. But he'll be wet and cold. Take my shawl.

(GRANDMA *hands* MRS. COLLINGWOOD *her shawl which has been lying folded on the back of a chair.* MRS. COLLINGWOOD *finally leaves.*)

MABEL

How many children do you suppose have fallen into that pond?

GRANDMA

All of you had more than one ducking, I'm sure.

127

MARY

Do you know I think Mrs. Collingwood would be nice if she could unbend a little.

GRANDMA

She's all right. I never pay any attention to people like that, and first thing you know they're real nice and friendly.

MABEL

Look at Mr. Timson. My goodness. He'd sleep right through an earthquake, wouldn't he?

MARY

Poor soul. I'm glad he got here for his Thanksgiving dinner. I'd better wake him up. (*Goes over and shakes* MR. TIMSON.) Mr. Timson, Mr. Timson. Wake up. It's nearly time for dinner.

(MR. TIMSON *opens his eyes and slowly sits up straight.*)

MR. TIMSON

I guess I must've dozed off for a little while.

GRANDMA

Yes, you did. And you missed all the excitement too. An automobile broke down, we have some visitors, and a little boy fell through the ice on the pond.

(MR. *and* MRS. COLLINGWOOD, DAN, LYNN *and all the children come in.* ROGER *is bundled up in* GRANDMA'S *shawl.*)

MR. COLLINGWOOD

Well here we are and no serious harm done.

ROGER

(*Proudly.*) I fell in the pond.

MRS. COLLINGWOOD

(*Sharply.*) Don't brag about it, Roger. You were lucky that the pond isn't deep.

128

MARY

What Roger needs now is dry clothes. George, take him upstairs and give him some of yours. We'll hang his in the kitchen by the stove so they can dry.

GEORGE

Come on, Roger. I'll fix you up.

(MRS. COLLINGWOOD, ROGER *and* GEORGE *start out the door.*)

ROGER

(*Suddenly stopping and speaking to his Mother.*) Where are you going?

MRS. COLLINGWOOD

With you, of course.

ROGER

No. Please don't. George and I'll manage, won't we George?

GEORGE

Sure we will.

MRS. COLLINGWOOD

I don't know about that.

ROGER

Aw, please, Mother.

MRS. COLLINGWOOD

Well, all right, but I want you to get those wet clothes off *immediately*. Do you understand?

(ROGER *and* GEORGE *run out.*)

ROGER

Wait 'till I tell the fellows at school how I almost drowned. They'll be jealous.

129

MARY

Don't you think you'd better accept Mother's invitation, Mrs. Collingwood? It'll take some time for Roger's clothes to dry.

MRS. COLLINGWOOD

I'm really terribly embarrassed. I still think it's too much to invite strangers to your Thanksgiving dinner.

GRANDMA

Stuff 'n' nonsense! I wouldn't have asked you if I hadn't wanted you.

MRS. COLLINGWOOD

(*Turning to husband.*) What do you think, Allan?

MR. COLLINGWOOD

You decide, my dear.

MRS. COLLINGWOOD

I shouldn't say "yes" but, I'd love it. Thank you very much.

MARY

Fine, now that's all settled. You people just lay your things in the parlor. It's right through the hall to your right. We keep that room closed off in the winter. We think it's cozier in here.
(MRS. COLLINGWOOD *leaves the room.*)

GRANDMA

And you children take off your coats and wash your hands. It'll soon be time for dinner.

RUTH

Come on kids. I'll show you where to put your things.
(*The children leave.*)

130

DAN

I'd like to take a look at that car of yours, Mr. Collingwood. Any objection?

MR. COLLINGWOOD

None at all. I'll be glad to show it to you.

LYNN

I'll come along too. Don't you want to see it, Mr. Timson?

MR. TIMSON

Don't mind if I do.
(*The four men leave as* MARY *calls after them.*)

MARY

Now don't be too long. Dinner will be ready soon. Tell Mr. Adams he'd better come in and get *his* hands washed too.
(MRS. COLLINGWOOD *comes in.*)

MRS. COLLINGWOOD

Is there anything I can do to help?

MARY

Thank you. Everything is all ready except for making the gravy.

MRS. COLLINGWOOD

(*Wistfully.*) I used to make good giblet gravy. When we were first married I was a good cook but I haven't done anything in the kitchen for years. I'd love to try my hand again. Could I?

MARY

Of course. Come on out in the kitchen. I'll get you an apron.
(MARY *and* MRS. COLLINGWOOD *leave.* MABEL *and* GRANDMA *look at each other.*)

131

MABEL

Well I never! Would you believe it?

GRANDMA

Of course I'd believe it. Now let's see, (*counting on her fingers.*) four more makes sixteen. Come on, Mabel, we need another leaf.
   (GRANDMA *and* MABEL *start clearing the table again.*)

MABEL

At least Mother, you had your wish. I wouldn't exactly call this a quiet Thanksgiving, would you?

(*curtain*)

thanksgiving at plymouth

JANETTE WOOLSEY

CHARACTERS

ELDER BREWSTER

GOVERNOR BRADFORD

SQUANTO

HOBOMUK

MASSASOIT

JOHN ALDEN

CAPTAIN STANDISH

INDIANS (*as many as wanted*)

MISTRESS BREWSTER

MISTRESS WINSLOW

HUMILITY COOPER (*8 years old*)

MARY CHILTON (*15 years old*)

PRISCILLA MULLINS

PILGRIM MEN AND CHILDREN
(*as many as wanted*)

COSTUMES

Women all wear long dresses, white neckpieces which fasten at waist, bonnets, aprons and capes. Men wear short trousers, jackets with wide collars, long stockings, broad-brimmed hats and capes. Indians wear khaki trunks, leggings and blankets which wrap around them. Their headbands have one or two feathers. Their faces are daubed with paint.

133

PROPERTIES

Table; stools; broom; dust cloth; rifles; ball; ping-pong paddles; badminton birds.

ACT ONE

TIME: *December, 1621.*

PLACE: *Interior of Common House at Plymouth. The furnishings are very simple. Table and stools are all that are necessary. When curtain opens,* PRISCILLA, MARY *and* HUMILITY *are sweeping and dusting.*

PRISCILLA

Humility, are you sure that you are getting the dust in all of the corners?

HUMILITY

Yes, I am, Priscilla. I have poked and poked and I'm sure there is not one speck of dust in any one of them.

PRISCILLA

There had better not be. Mistress Winslow has a very sharp eye and she wants us to have this room spotless. Governor Bradford, Captain Standish and Elder Brewster are meeting in it this very morning.

MARY

I wish I were dusting my own house. Do you not wish for one too, Priscilla?

PRISCILLA

Of course I do, Mary. But no doubt you will be mistress of one

134

when you are older. Until then you should be thankful that Mistress Brewster has given you a home with her.

HUMILITY

Well, I'm glad to be dusting. (*Sighing.*) Taking care of little children is hard work.

PRISCILLA

That it is, I know. But think what would those motherless children have done if Mistress Brewster had not offered to help Isaac Allerton after he was left with three to care for?

HUMILITY

You're right. I shouldn't complain, because she's taking care of me, too.

MARY

(*Slowly.*) Priscilla, are you going to marry Captain Miles Standish?

PRISCILLA

(*Stopping her work and speaking indignantly.*) Mary Chilton! What a thing to ask!

MARY

(*Defensively.*) Well, I thought perhaps you were. I heard Mistress Winslow and Mistress Brewster discussing it the other day.

HUMILITY

I heard them too, Priscilla. Mary and I were both there when they were talking. We like John Alden better, don't we, Mary?

PRISCILLA

(*Sharply.*) You had no right to listen and certainly if you did listen, you should never repeat anything you hear.

MARY

Well, I only wondered.

PRISCILLA

You just stop wondering.

HUMILITY

Oh, all right. But John Alden is nice. Truly he is.

MARY

I'm sorry, Priscilla. Forgive me, please.

PRISCILLA

(*Suddenly melting.*) Of course I do. (*Hesitatingly.*) And—to tell the truth—I think John Alden is nice, too.

HUMILITY

Priscilla, before we go couldn't you tell us once more about our home in England?

MARY

I don't remember living there at all.

PRISCILLA

(*Slowly.*) We shouldn't stay here now that our work is finished. 'Tis a sin to be idle and (*Teasingly*) anyway I'm not sure I should after what you said to me.

HUMILITY

(*Pleadingly.*) Please, Priscilla?

PRISCILLA

(*Laughing.*) Oh, well—but just for a few minutes and no longer. (*She seats herself on a stool and* MARY *and* HUMILITY *sit on the floor at her feet.*) It seems a long time ago and yet I remember it

136

all so well. I was only six when we left England to go to Holland. And I remember you too, Mary. You were three.

HUMILITY

(*Eagerly.*) And do you remember me too, Priscilla?

PRISCILLA

(*Gently and patting* HUMILITY *on the head.*) You know I don't. You weren't born until we had been in Holland several years.

MARY

(*Impatiently.*) Do go on, Priscilla. I want to hear about England.

PRISCILLA

We lived in a little village close by a moor which was almost overgrown with heather.

HUMILITY

What is heather?

MARY

(*Quickly.*) You've been told a hundred times, Humility. It's a purplish flower. Now don't interrupt again.

PRISCILLA

(*Dreamily.*) Right from our dooryard you could look out and see the hills. I remember them because I used to think that the world ended there. It was as far as I could see.

HUMILITY

And your house, Priscilla. Tell us about that.

PRISCILLA

I only remember a little about that. It had a fireplace, I know, because I can close my eyes and still see the andirons. Once I crawled too close to them and got burned. I still have the scar. See?
(*She holds up her arm.*)

137

IT'S TIME FOR THANKSGIVING

HUMILITY

Now tell me about Holland where I was born.

PRISCILLA

(*Chidingly.*) Humility! You remember Holland as well as I do. I declare I think you are just wanting to waste time. (*Jumping up.*) We must go. Here comes Governor Bradford. Hurry!

(PRISCILLA, MARY *and* HUMILITY *gather up the broom and dust cloths and leave. They meet* GOVERNOR BRADFORD, CAPTAIN STANDISH *and* ELDER BREWSTER *as they reach the door. The girls make brief curtsies as they pass the men.* GOVERNOR BRADFORD, CAPTAIN STANDISH *and* ELDER BREWSTER *seat themselves at the table.*)

GOVERNOR BRADFORD

I have asked you here, Captain Standish, to discuss a plan that Elder Brewster has for making the Indians even closer friends with us than they are now.

CAPTAIN STANDISH

That sounds interesting, Governor Bradford. Chief Massasoit and his braves have been friendly but I, too, think we should do more to assure them that we intend no harm to them.

GOVERNOR BRADFORD

I don't think anything ever surprised me more than the Indian, Samoset, saying, "Welcome," when we landed.

ELDER BREWSTER

And it is important that all our Indian friends continue to say, "Welcome" to us.

CAPTAIN STANDISH

We have been most fortunate that Squanto and Hobomuk have wanted to live here in Plymouth with us. I'm sure it has done much to keep the Indians at peace.

138

GOVERNOR BRADFORD

I can't say that I blame them for preferring Plymouth to their Indian village. After all Squanto was in Europe and is familiar with our way of living. But right now there have been rumors of Indian uprisings elsewhere. Elder Brewster and I think we should be sure that Massasoit is on our side.

CAPTAIN STANDISH

What do you have in mind, Governor?

GOVERNOR BRADFORD

It is Elder Brewster's plan, so I'll let him explain it to you.

ELDER BREWSTER

Well, this is the harvest season. Our crops are in and they have been bountiful. I propose that we have a Thanksgiving feast day and invite our Indian friends to partake of it with us.

CAPTAIN STANDISH

I feel sure that they would like that.
(JOHN ALDEN *enters.*)

JOHN ALDEN

Good morning. May I interrupt for a moment?

GOVERNOR BRADFORD

You are always welcome, John Alden. I hope though that you do not bring bad news of any kind.

JOHN ALDEN

Oh, no. I wanted to tell you that another house is completed and is ready for whatever family you decide to assign to it.

GOVERNOR BRADFORD

That is good news, John. We're fortunate to have two such excellent carpenters as you and Francis Eaton as members of our colony. I shall attend to that matter shortly. Right now Captain Standish and I are discussing Elder Brewster's plan for a day of Thanksgiving.

JOHN ALDEN

That sounds interesting, Governor.

GOVERNOR BRADFORD

Do you know if Squanto and Hobomuk are anywhere in the village? I'd like very much to see them.

JOHN ALDEN

I'll go find them and send them to you.
(JOHN ALDEN *leaves.*)

CAPTAIN STANDISH

That's a fine young man. He seems like one to be trusted.

GOVERNOR BRADFORD

I'm sure he is.

ELDER BREWSTER

I hope the next ship from England will bring more young men like him. Our colony needs men of courage and of skill.
(SQUANTO *and* HOBOMUK *enter.*)

SQUANTO

We met John Alden outside the door and he says you want to see us.

GOVERNOR BRADFORD

Yes, I do. I'd like to have you, Squanto and you, Hobomuk, go to Chief Massasoit and invite him to come to Plymouth and enjoy our Thanksgiving feast with us.

HOBOMUK

Thanksgiving? What is that?

140

GOVERNOR BRADFORD

It's a celebration in honor of the good fortune which has befallen us. When we were in Leyden, Holland, the people of that city celebrated in memory of the time when the Spaniards were driven from their country. We wish to celebrate because we have had an abundant harvest and will have food to last us this coming winter.

ELDER BREWSTER

And we wish to share our feast with Chief Massasoit.

SQUANTO

We'll go as you ask. Massasoit will come I'm sure.
(SQUANTO *and* HOBOMUK *leave.*)

GOVERNOR BRADFORD

And now we must tell the women so that they may begin to prepare our Thanksgiving feast.

(*curtain*)

ACT TWO

TIME: *A few days later.*
PLACE: *A clearing near the Plymouth Common House.*
(*When the curtain opens* MISTRESS WINSLOW, MISTRESS BREWSTER *and* PRISCILLA *are on stage.*)

MISTRESS BREWSTER

This has been a hard three days.

MISTRESS WINSLOW

(*Sighing deeply.*) I'm thankful it'll soon be over.

PRISCILLA

I'm still having a hard time convincing myself that what I saw actually happened.

MISTRESS WINSLOW

We should have a Thanksgiving now to celebrate the fact that we don't have to cook for that many all the time.

PRISCILLA

When I saw Chief Massasoit walk into this village with ninety Indian braves I could hardly believe my eyes.

MISTRESS BREWSTER

Such appetites! Their squaws must have to cook all the time!

MISTRESS WINSLOW

I kept wondering, what shall we do? Our food will never hold out.

142

PRISCILLA

(*Laughing.*) But they turned out to be good guests after all. I certainly was relieved when Massasoit sent them out to secure more food. Let's see—how many deer did they bring back with them?

MISTRESS WINSLOW

I think it was five.

MISTRESS BREWSTER

(*Dryly.*) At least we know they are enjoying themselves. This is the third day they've been here.

MISTRESS WINSLOW

Governor Bradford must feel very satisfied. I'm sure our men have managed to convince Massasoit and his Indians that we want to be friendly.

MISTRESS BREWSTER

Yes, I hope I'll be able to sleep easy again. Ever since we had the trouble with Chief Corbitant I've feared that he'd some day attack us.

PRISCILLA

Governor Bardford says he's sure that Corbitant is afraid of our muskets. But just the same it's a good feeling to know that Massasoit is our friend.

MISTRESS WINSLOW

Here they all come now. They must be finished eating at last. Come, we have work to do. The trenchers must be cleaned so that they will be ready for the next meal. And we must see that the children are fed, too.

PRISCILLA

Poor little ones. They've been really neglected these past few days, haven't they?

MISTRESS BREWSTER

I must say that Humility Cooper has been a wondrous help. She's not only cared for the three Allerton children but she's had to tend the Eaton baby too. She's going to turn out to be a responsible girl after all.

PRISCILLA

Oh, Humility is fine. She's bright and quick. I'm very fond of her.

(*As the women are talking they move off the stage in one direction as the men come on in another.* GOVERNOR BRADFORD, ELDER BREWSTER, CAPTAIN STANDISH, JOHN ALDEN, SQUANTO, HOBOMUK, CHIEF MASSASOIT *and other* PILGRIMS *and* INDIANS *enter.*)

GOVERNOR BRADFORD

Here's a good spot. We can stop here.

SQUANTO

Chief Massasoit asks if white men want to see his braves wrestle.

GOVERNOR BRADFORD

Yes indeed we do. (*Turning to* CAPTAIN STANDISH.) Although how they can wrestle after all they've eaten, I don't know!

(*Two pairs of* INDIANS *prepare to wrestle. They lie down in opposite directions close to one another. They lock right legs and right arms and then try to roll each other over. The* PILGRIMS *stand around and cheer them on. The other* INDIANS *stand watching with their arms folded. After the wrestling is over* GOVERNOR BRADFORD *speaks.*)

GOVERNOR BRADFORD

Captain Standish, have our men give an exhibition of a military review.

CAPTAIN STANDISH

Very well, Governor. Attention, men! Fall in! Shoulder arms! (*The* PILGRIMS *form a line, muskets on shoulders. As* CAPTAIN

144

STANDISH *calls out the commands they drill according to orders.*)
Right face! Forward march! In place! Halt! To the rear! Forward
march! In place, halt! Right face! As you were!

(*The men break formation. When the drilling is over the* INDIANS,
with the exception of MASSASOIT, SQUANTO *and* HOBOMUK, *begin
to kick a ball around. The* PILGRIMS *with the exception of* GOVERNOR
BRADFORD, ELDER BREWSTER *and* CAPTAIN STANDISH *join them. Next
they play Shuttlecock and Battledore. This may be played with a
badminton bird and ping-pong paddles. The players stand in a circle
and pass the bird from one to another without letting it touch the
ground. As they play* HOBOMUK *is seen talking to* MASSASOIT.)

HOBOMUK

Chief Massasoit is pleased that white men play games with his
braves.

GOVERNOR BRADFORD

Tell the chief that this game is much like one we used to play in
England. It's good for our men to act young again and to enjoy
themselves.

SQUANTO

He's glad because he thought that the white man cared for nothing
but work.

CAPTAIN STANDISH

Work is necessary so that one can live. But we know how to enter
into a game, too.

(*The game finally stops.* MASSASOIT *and his* INDIANS *prepare to
leave.*)

SQUANTO

Chief Massasoit and his warriors say good-by.

(INDIANS *and* PILGRIMS *hold up their hands in good-by salutes
and the* INDIANS *file out in a single line led by* MASSASOIT.)

145

CAPTAIN STANDISH

I believe that Chief Massasoit and his braves are really our friends.

GOVERNOR BRADFORD

I feel sure that they are. But now there is one more thing to do. (*Turning to one of the* PILGRIMS.) Call the women and ask them to come here. (*The man leaves and returns immediately with the women and girls.*) Now that our feasting is over there remains one thing. (*Turning to* ELDER BREWSTER.)

ELDER BREWSTER

We should not forget Him to whom we owe all our blessings. It is fitting before we end our days of feasting that once again we all give thanks to God who has brought us safely to the beginning of a new year in this land.

(*The* PILGRIMS *all stand with bowed heads and say the next speech in unison.*)

ALL TOGETHER

"Enter into his gates with thanksgiving, and into his courts with praise: be thankful unto him, and bless his name."

(*As the* PILGRIMS *remain standing on the stage the* DIRECTOR *of the play steps forward and asks the audience all to join together in singing the first and last stanzas of* AMERICA.)

(*curtain*)

146

a postponed thanksgiving

JANETTE WOOLSEY

CHARACTERS

MRS. ALLEN	GOVERNOR BRADFORD
MR. ALLEN	MILES STANDISH
JANE, *their daughter*	FIRST PILGRIM MAN
TED, *their son*	SECOND PILGRIM MAN
NEWSCASTER	PILGRIM WOMAN
WEATHER MAN	PILGRIM CHILD

COSTUMES

The Allen family wear ordinary clothes. JANE *and* TED *wear bathrobes in the early part of the scene. The* PILGRIMS *wear traditional Pilgrim costumes but no cloaks since their scene occurs in the middle of a very hot season.*

PROPERTIES

Living room furniture which includes an artificial fireplace; radio; record player which is used off-stage; wood for fireplace;

147

card table; luncheon cloth; napkins; silver; tray; four glasses of orange juice; other dishes; telephone.

TIME: *The present. Thanksgiving Day.*

PLACE: *The living room of the* ALLEN *family. There is a fireplace at the rear of the stage and chairs are grouped near it. A table with a lamp is near by. When the curtain opens it is quite dark on stage.* MR. ALLEN *is standing at an open door looking out.* MRS. ALLEN *enters and goes over to the table and turns on the light. Stage lights come on at the same time.*

MRS. ALLEN

Brrr. It's cold in here. John, why in the world are you standing there with the door wide open?

MR. ALLEN

(*Closing door and coming toward* MRS. ALLEN.) Sorry, dear, I didn't think what I was doing. I was just looking out at the driveway and road.

MRS. ALLEN

It looks pretty bad, doesn't it?

MR. ALLEN

(*Emphatically.*) Awful! The streets are a mass of ice and there seems to be no let-up in this downpour of sleet.

MRS. ALLEN

It certainly seems strange not to hear any cars.

MR. ALLEN

Well, no one in his right mind would be out on a morning like this. Are the children awake?

148

MRS. ALLEN

They weren't when I looked in their rooms a few minutes ago. I didn't want to wake them up until we had a chance to discuss what we're going to do.

MR. ALLEN

I'm afraid there's not going to be much to discuss. I don't think it's going to be possible to stir out of this driveway today, let alone take a sixty mile ride.

MRS. ALLEN

I suppose not. But how I hate to break the news to Jane and Ted! They look forward to Thanksgiving at their grandmother's more than anything else.

MR. ALLEN

I know, and it's a shame. But I have a feeling that this storm is pretty wide-spread, and if I know your mother she won't want us to try it either.

MRS. ALLEN

I'm sure she won't.
(*Voices are heard off-stage.*)

JANE

Get up, Ted, you old sleepyhead. You'll miss Thanksgiving if you don't.

TED

I'm up. I'll race you downstairs, Janie.
(JANE *and* TED *enter on a run. They are both wearing bathrobes.*)

JANE

Good morning, Mother. Good morning, Daddy. Oh, boy! Am I excited! When do we start? Are we going to leave for Grandma's right after breakfast?

TED

Good morning, everybody. Say, what's the matter? You two look sort of glum.

MR. ALLEN

Sorry, youngsters, we have bad news for you.

JANE

What's the trouble, Daddy? (*Turning to* MOTHER.) What is it? Are you sick, Mother?

MRS. ALLEN

No, Janie. But look out of the window.
(*Both children rush to the window.*)

TED

Oh, no! It can't be. It just can't!

JANE

It's ice, isn't it? Solid ice all over everything—and it's still coming down.

MR. ALLEN

I guess you both know what that means, don't you?

JANE

(*Nodding her head slowly.*) You mean we can't go to Grandma's for Thanksgiving, don't you? Oh, I can't bear it.
  (JANE *runs over to the couch and throws herself on it, burying her head in the pillows.*)

TED

(*Hopefully.*) Maybe it'll clear off soon. Don't you think it will, Dad?

150

MR. ALLEN

I don't know, of course. But from the looks of it and from the feel of the temperature outside, I have my doubts.

(MRS. ALLEN *goes over to* JANE *and sits down beside her.*)

MRS. ALLEN

Now come, Janie. I'm disappointed, too. You know I've always spent Thanksgiving at my old home and it's hard not to go. But you're not going to let this spoil the day for all of us, are you?

(JANE *lifts her head and sniffs audibly.*)

JANE

N-no. I guess not. Have you called Grandma?

MR. ALLEN

Not yet. I thought we'd hear the weather report first. What time is it? (*Looks at watch.*) Seven-ten. Ted, will you turn the radio on? I hope we haven't missed it.

(TED *goes over to the radio and turns it on. A voice is heard just finishing a news broadcast.*)

NEWSCASTER

And that concludes the news from our nation, our state and our town. And now the person you all want to hear on this cold blustery Thanksgiving morning—the weather man!

WEATHER MAN

Good morning, folks, if you can call it a good morning. Thanksgiving arrived this morning with freezing temperatures and a freezing rain. And for all of you people who were planning to be on the highways this morning, my advice is—don't! Here is the bad news. The drop in temperature will last most of the day becoming somewhat milder late this afternoon. Rain is slated for this entire section of the state, due to end in the early evening. Tomorrow's forecast calls for sunny skies and moderate tem-

151

perature. I'll give you the details after this brief word from our sponsor.

(JANE *runs over and turns the radio off.*)

JANE

(*Vehemently.*) I don't want to hear one more word. (*Stamping her foot.*) I'm just so mad—mad—mad!

MRS. ALLEN

(*Sternly.*) Now Jane! It's not going to help to lose your temper and you're being very childish. John, we'd better call Mother right away, don't you think?

MR. ALLEN

Right you are. (*He goes over to the telephone and dials the operator.*) Hello, I'd like to place a call to Sunnyburn. The number is four–seven–R–three. (*Pause.*) Oh, the lines are down? Ice on them, did you say? (*Pause.*) Yes, I'd like to leave the call in. My number is seven–six–five–four. Thank you very much.

MRS. ALLEN

Can't you get through?

MR. ALLEN

Not now. Apparently the ice was too much for some of the lines. The operator says that repairmen are working on them and she'll call me as soon as she can put our call through.

TED

I'm glad I'm not a repairman. That wouldn't be easy today, would it?

MR. ALLEN

It sure wouldn't. But we should be thankful that there are people who are willing to sacrifice their own comfort to help us.

152

MRS. ALLEN

May I make a suggestion? No long faces today, please. Let's all have a good time together. We have much to be thankful for. See how much more we have than lots of people all over the world.

JANE

I'm sorry, truly I am. (*Wistfully.*) But I keep thinking about that Thanksgiving turkey that Grandma has.

MR. ALLEN

If it's nice we can go Saturday. (*Laughing.*) There may still be a few bones for you to pick.

JANE

But Thanksgiving isn't the same if you don't have it on the right day.

MR. ALLEN

Of course it is. It doesn't make a bit of difference what day you celebrate it on. Don't you know that the second Thanksgiving was celebrated on the thirtieth of July?

TED

The thirtieth of July? No, I never heard that, Dad. How did it happen?

JANE

(*Eagerly.*) Tell us, Daddy. I don't remember reading that in my history book.

MRS. ALLEN

Now wait just a minute, please, before you begin a story. I'd like to hear it too, but I'm hungry. How about the rest of you?

153

MR. ALLEN

(*Laughing.*) I knew something was wrong besides the weather, but I couldn't figure out what. Hot food is what I need.

MRS. ALLEN

Jane, you and Ted go up and get dressed. Dad, if you'll build a fire in the fireplace we can have breakfast right here where it's cozy and warm. How would you all like that?

JANE

(*Throwing her arms around her mother.*) I'd love it—and I'm sorry I was such a baby.

MRS. ALLEN

(*Giving her a little pat.*) That's all right, dear. It is disappointing but it won't be too bad and we'll still have Thanksgiving to look forward to. (*Turning to the others.*) How would you like waffles and sausage this morning?

TED

(*Shouting.*) How would we? Just ask us. Come on, Janie. I'll race you getting dressed.

(TED and JANE *run off the stage.*)

MR. ALLEN

Whew! Such energy! Do you think the four walls will hold together for a whole day?

MRS. ALLEN

I hope so! And do you know, dear, I think it's going to be nice for all of us to have a day together. It hasn't happened in a long, long time.

MR. ALLEN

We can make it a real Thanksgiving.

154

MRS. ALLEN

I never heard the story of the second Thanksgiving either. Did it really come on the thirtieth of July?

MR. ALLEN

It really did. And as soon as we're ready for breakfast I'll tell the story.

MRS. ALLEN

I'm as eager as the children. Get the fire made, dear. I won't be long. We'll have our breakfast and "The Second Thanksgiving" in just a few minutes.

(MRS. ALLEN *leaves the room.* MR. ALLEN *starts to poke around in the fireplace.* JANE *and* TED *enter.*)

JANE

See, I told you that girls are as fast as boys.

TED

I'll bet you cheated. Sure you didn't have any clothes on under that bathrobe?

JANE

(*Airily.*) Oh, maybe, just a teensy-weensy few.

TED

(*Disgustedly.*) I thought so. (*Turning to* MR. ALLEN.) Need some help, Dad?

MR. ALLEN

Well, you might go down cellar and bring up some wood. And don't forget a few sticks of kindling.

(TED *leaves the room.* JANE *goes over to the radio and turns it on. Recorded popular song is heard.* JANE *begins dancing around humming to herself.* MRS. ALLEN *enters with a luncheon cloth in her hand.*)

155

MRS. ALLEN

Janie, how about setting the table? You may use this cloth.

(MRS. ALLEN *hands* JANE *the cloth then leaves the room.* JANE *goes over and gets a card table, sets it up and begins to set the table. She still continues to keep time to the music and hum as she does it.* TED *returns with the wood and* MR. ALLEN *fixes the fire.* MRS. ALLEN *enters carrying a tray with four glasses of orange juice on it.*)

MRS. ALLEN

Here's the first course. Let's have our orange juice while we're waiting for the waffles.

TED

M-m-m. They sure smell good—or maybe it's the sausage. Anyway, I'm hungry.

JANE

So am I!

(*They all sit down and take each other's hands around the table as they bow their heads for a moment. Then as they raise their heads and begin to drink their juice* MRS. ALLEN *speaks.*)

MRS. ALLEN

Now, how about beginning that story, John?

TED

Oh, yes. I almost forgot.

JANE

I didn't. I was going to remind Dad. Did you say it was the thirtieth of July the Pilgrims celebrated Thanksgiving?

MR. ALLEN

Yes. You see it happened like this—

156

(The stage is darkened for a minute. When the lights go on two PILGRIMS *are standing at the side of the stage. During the next scene the* ALLENS *sit quietly watching the* PILGRIMS.)

FIRST PILGRIM

The sky is overcast again today. It may mean that we'll have more rain.

SECOND PILGRIM

If it hadn't been for the rain last week I don't think our colony could have lasted the summer.

FIRST PILGRIM

You're right. Day after day of that parching heat was almost more than I could bear. To see my crops dying was frightening. Not many of us could have endured it much longer.

SECOND PILGRIM

Governor Bradford did well to appoint a day last week for fasting and prayer, and the rains that came in answer were like a miracle.

FIRST PILGRIM

Yes, it was a miracle to see the corn come to life again and to know that we still have a chance to survive.
  (PILGRIM WOMAN *enters.*)

PILGRIM WOMAN

Have you seen Governor Bradford?

SECOND PILGRIM

Not for some time. Is anything wrong?

PILGRIM WOMAN

No. I saw him go down to the shore this morning. I thought he might have returned with some news of Captain Miles Standish.

157

FIRST PILGRIM

It's been a long time since Captain Standish set sail to bring us new supplies. I hope nothing has happened to his ship.

SECOND PILGRIM

Captain Standish is a brave man. He will get that ship back at all costs, I know.

(PILGRIM BOY *runs in.*)

PILGRIM BOY

(*Shouting.*) The ship is in! The ship is in! Captain Standish has returned!

PILGRIM WOMAN

(*Fervently.*) Let us give thanks that he has been brought safely home again.

(GOVERNOR BRADFORD *and* CAPTAIN MILES STANDISH *enter.*)

FIRST PILGRIM

It is indeed a welcome sight to see you, Captain Standish.

CAPTAIN STANDISH

The voyage was not an easy one, but we have all survived and for that we are grateful.

GOVERNOR BRADFORD

And were you able to get the supplies we need, Captain Standish?

CAPTAIN STANDISH

Yes, Governor Bradford, I was. But tell me, what has happened since I left Plymouth?

GOVERNOR BRADFORD

When you left it seemed as though our colony had come upon sad times, Captain. Because of this summer's dry weather our corn

158

was scorched and our beans were stunted. But we didn't lose faith. We believed that we would survive.

CAPTAIN STANDISH

But the corn looks good. I noticed it as I came up from the ship. Not as good as the first crop we planted, perhaps, but still there is one.

PILGRIM WOMAN

Our prayers were answered, Captain Standish.

FIRST PILGRIM

Governor Bradford called us together, to pray. And for nine hours we did so.

SECOND PILGRIM

And our prayers were answered with a rain which revived our crops.

CAPTAIN STANDISH

And I have more good news for you. We sighted a ship from Holland which should be here soon. I'm sure it's bringing fresh supplies and friends who will want to settle in our colony.

GOVERNOR BRADFORD

This is indeed good news!

PILGRIM WOMAN

(*Clasping her hands.*) It is a time for Thanksgiving.

GOVERNOR BRADFORD

And I shall declare one. Let us all gather together tomorrow, the thirtieth day of July, in the Year of our Lord, 1623, and rejoice that we have again been delivered from our troubles and misfortunes. We shall give thanks in acknowledgment of all our great blessings.

159

(Stage is darkened. During this time the PILGRIMS *leave. Some-one quietly places more dishes on the breakfast table so that it will look as though the* ALLENS *had finished eating. When the lights come on* JANE *speaks.)*

JANE

My, that certainly is interesting, Daddy.

MRS. ALLEN

Yes, it is. It's hard to realize what a difficult life our ancestors had.

TED

Sounds pretty rugged to me. I've always thought it would've been fun to have lived at that time. But now I'm not quite so sure.

JANE

(Emphatically.) I'm sure. I know I wouldn't. Think of not having enough to eat, being afraid of Indians and all the wild animals, too.

MR. ALLEN

They were willing to risk all that because they believed so strongly in the right to worship as they pleased. We should always be grateful to them.

MRS. ALLEN

Just last week I was reading the story of the first Thanksgiving to my Girl Scouts. It said that the four women of the colony had to prepare and cook enough food for three days for one hundred and twenty men, and that ninety of these were Indians with enormous appetites.

JANE

I wonder what they had to eat.

MRS. ALLEN

According to Governor Bradford's account, the Pilgrims provided wild turkeys, shellfish and eels, and the Indians brought five deer.

160

JANE

Eels? Ugh! Imagine having eels for Thanksgiving!

TED

They'd have loved your waffles and sausages, Mom.

MRS. ALLEN

Thank you, Ted. Would anyone like more?

MR. ALLEN

They were excellent. But no more, thank you.

JANE

I scarcely knew I was eating them I was so interested in Dad's story. But I'm full to the brim so I must have eaten plenty.

TED

(*Slyly.*) Better be careful, Janie, or you won't have room for turkey.

JANE

(*Indignantly.*) Now, Ted. No joking about that, please. But after Dad's story I should be thankful to be full of waffles.

MRS. ALLEN

Now, let's see. We'll have to make a few new plans. Jane, would you like to help me make a mince pie?

JANE

(*Jumping up.*) Oh, yes! Are we going to begin now?

MRS. ALLEN

As soon as we get the other work done. (*Telephone rings.*) Oh, that must be Mother.

161

IT'S TIME FOR THANKSGIVING

MR. ALLEN

(*Answering phone.*) Hello. (*Pause.*) Good morning, Mother. We tried to get you about an hour and a half ago but the lines were down. Here's Helen. She wants to talk with you.

MRS. ALLEN

(*Taking phone.*) Hello Mother. (*Pause.*) Yes, it's very bad here, too. (*Pause.*) I was sure you wouldn't expect us. (*Pause.*) Yes, we're disappointed, too. The children were very unhappy. (*Pause.*) Well, we've talked it over and John says that if you want us, we can drive over Saturday morning and stay until Sunday. (*Pause.*) That's good news. Janie was especially worried about that. Here she is. You tell her.

JANE

(*Taking phone.*) Hello, Grandma. (*Pause.*) Didn't you even put the turkey in the oven this morning? (*Turning to others and smiling broadly.*) She says she had a feeling in her bones when she woke up that we wouldn't make it. (*Talking to her grandmother again.*) We'll save our appetites for Saturday. Give my love to Grandpa. Wait a minute. Here's Ted.

TED

(*Taking phone.*) Say, Grandma. Did you know we'll be like the Pilgrims celebrating Thanksgiving another day? They celebrated it once on the thirtieth of July. (*Pause.*) No, I'm not kidding. You can ask my dad. He told us about it this morning. (*Pause.*) Yes, I'll tell them. Good-by.

(TED *hangs up the receiver and turns to the others.*)

TED

She sends her love and says she'll expect us Saturday. Say, Mom, if Janie helps you with the mince pie, what can I do?

162

MRS. ALLEN

Crack some nuts and then you and Jane can stuff some dates.

MR. ALLEN

And where do I come in on these big preparations?

TED

Oh, you keep the home fires burning. And say, how about playing a game of chess with me later?

MR. ALLEN

Fine. We'll do that.

JANE

(*Suddenly.*) I've just been thinking of all the things I'm thankful for. I'm thankful first of all for the brave Pilgrims for their first Thanksgiving and for the second one, too. But most of all I'm thankful for my family, and that when it's sleety and blustery outside we're cozy and warm together in here. Oh, (*Clapping her hands and twirling around.*) I'm thankful for everything! Come on, Mother, let's get that mince pie started.

(*curtain*)

how autumn came to the earth

JANETTE WOOLSEY

CHARACTERS

NARRATOR	LITTLE GIRL
PROSERPINA	YOUNG MAN
NYMPHS (5)	WOMAN
PLUTO	ARETHUSA
CERES	JUPITER
OLD MAN	MERCURY

MEN *and* WOMEN (*As many as desired*)

COSTUMES

GIRLS *all wear long, full sleeveless dresses with wide girdles belting them in at the waist.* BOYS *wear short tunics. Over this is worn a mantle which covers one shoulder and is fastened on the other. It is designed so that it falls down both front and back.*

PROPERTIES

Baskets with flower petals; staff for Ceres; cart with wood.
(*When the curtain opens the* NARRATOR *is standing at the side of the stage.* NARRATOR'S *part may be read.*)

164

NARRATOR

This is the time of year when all over America people are enjoying the Thanksgiving celebration. All of us know that Thanksgiving was first observed in this country when our Pilgrim fore-
fathers set aside a day for feasting and rejoicing. They were
thankful that the abundance of their crops that fall had provided
enough food to see them through the cold winter days ahead. But
the idea of a Thanksgiving day was not a new one to the Pilgrims.
Down through the centuries various peoples had observed such
a day in memory of some particular event. In Leyden, Holland,
where the Pilgrims had lived before setting sail in the *Mayflower*
for a new land, they had seen the Hollanders celebrating a Thanksgiving day in remembrance of their victory over Spain in 1575.
But long before that time the ancient Romans had celebrated a
Thanksgiving. The Romans believed in many gods and goddesses
and had certain days which were sacred to them. Ceres was the
Goddess of the Harvest and the Roman festival in her honor was
called the Feast of Cerelia. It is her story we are going to tell to
you now. Our play begins on the shores of a lake in the vale of
Enna where Proserpina, daughter of the Goddess, Ceres, is playing
with some of her companions.

(*Lights are darkened.* NARRATOR *leaves stage. When lights come
on* PROSERPINA *and* NYMPHS *enter dancing. Small baskets filled
with flower petals are suspended from their necks by ribbons. A
ballet dance can be used here with a recording of Debussy's "Afternoon of a Faun" played off-stage for background music. As they
dance they scatter the petals. At the conclusion of the dance* PROSER-
PINA *throws herself on the ground.*)

PROSERPINA

(*Laughing.*) Stop! Stop! I'm breathless. I can dance no longer.
    (*The* NYMPHS *sit down grouped around* PROSERPINA. *They take
their baskets off and place them on the ground.*)

165

FIRST NYMPH

I'm tired too. We've wandered far away from home today. Do you not think we should soon be going back?

SECOND NYMPH

Perhaps your mother the Goddess Ceres will be alarmed over your long absence, Proserpina.

PROSERPINA

(*Carelessly.*) I'm sure she won't. My mother is busy visiting the fields to see that the crops of the mortals will be abundant this year.

THIRD NYMPH

You must be very proud of her. She brings happiness to so many people.

FOURTH NYMPH

I have heard that she worships you, Proserpina, just as mortals worship her.

PROSERPINA

Yes, she does. But sometimes I wish she wouldn't be so watchful. She never wants me to be out of her sight. That's why I enjoy a carefree day like this so much.

FIFTH NYMPH

We nymphs are happy that you chose us to be your companions today, but I really fear you should return to your mother's home.

PROSERPINA

(*Jumping to her feet.*) In a little while! But first let's dance once more. I'm rested now.

(*The* NYMPHS *get up and join her, leaving their baskets on the ground. Suddenly off-stage there is a rumbling, thundery sound.*

166

The lights go off and then come on again immediately. PROSERPINA
and the NYMPHS *stand there paralyzed with fear.*)

FIRST NYMPH

Wh-what was that?

PROSERPINA

(*Reassuringly.*) 'Tis nothing. Just a summer storm to bring needed
moisture to the earth.
    (*The rumbling is heard again.*)

SECOND NYMPH

I'm frightened! It sounds like no storm I've ever heard before.

THIRD NYMPH

I'm frightened too. Let's go quickly before some evil befalls us.

PROSERPINA

(*Shading her eyes with her hand and looking off.*) Look! A chariot
is approaching drawn by four horses as black as the night.

FIRST NYMPH

(*Quickly.*) Come Proserpina! It's Pluto, ruler of the Underworld!
Hurry!
    (*The* NYMPHS *and* PROSERPINA *run off. Then* PROSERPINA *runs
back on stage toward her basket of flowers.*)

PROSERPINA

(*Calling.*) I forgot my flowers.
    (*Just as* PROSERPINA *picks up her basket,* PLUTO *rushes in and
seizes her.* PROSERPINA *screams and struggles to get free.*)

PLUTO

Stop, Proserpina, stop! I have no intention of harming you.

167

PROSERPINA

(*Crying.*) Then let me go.

PLUTO

For a long time I've wanted you to rule the Underworld with me as my queen. But never before have I seen you without your mother, Ceres, close by.

PROSERPINA

(*Still struggling to free herself.*) Oh, would that my mother were here now!

PLUTO

Come, come, Proserpina. Don't struggle. My chariot is waiting and my four noble horses are impatient to be gone.

(PLUTO *drags* PROSERPINA *across the stage. The* NYMPHS *have run in from the other side and are standing with their arms outstretched toward* PROSERPINA. *She tries once more to release herself from* PLUTO's *grasp.*)

PROSERPINA

Help! Help! Mother Ceres! Where are you? Help me! Help me!

(*As* PLUTO *and* PROSERPINA *reach the edge of the stage the girdle which binds her dress at the waist drops off and falls unnoticed to the ground. Lights darken for a moment and when they come on again* PLUTO *and* PROSERPINA *have left stage and* NARRATOR *is standing at the side.*)

NARRATOR

When Proserpina did not return home, her mother Ceres started out to look for her. Day and night she wandered over the face of the earth searching for her daughter. Proserpina's playmates, the Nymphs, terrified that Ceres would blame them for Proserpina's misfortune, returned to their home. As our story continues we find Ceres still looking for Proserpina.

(*Lights darken.* NARRATOR *leaves. Lights come on again.* CERES *enters. She carries a staff in her hand.*)

CERES

Proserpina! Proserpina! My daughter, answer me.

(*An* OLD MAN *and* LITTLE GIRL *enter dragging a cart filled with sticks of wood.*)

CERES

Old man, have you seen my daughter?

OLD MAN

I'm sorry. I do not know you or your daughter.

CERES

(*Proudly.*) I am the Goddess Ceres, and I have lost my daughter, Proserpina. I appear to you in human form to ask your help.

OLD MAN

(*Falling to his knees.*) Your forgiveness, most gracious Goddess. Long have I worshiped you and given thanks for your bounty to me and my family.

CERES

You need not kneel. But I do want an answer to my question. Have you seen my daughter? It's been weeks since she disappeared.

OLD MAN

I don't know if this has anything to do with your daughter's disappearance but I do remember an unusual happening. Some weeks ago I was coming home from my field when I thought I heard a young girl's cry for help. I rushed toward the place where the sound came from. I found no one, but there was a huge opening in the ground. Just as I got there the opening slowly closed, but near by I picked this up.

169

(*The* OLD MAN *motions to the* LITTLE GIRL *who takes from her waist the girdle which* PROSERPINA *had dropped and hands it to* CERES. CERES *examines it closely.*)

CERES

(*Excitedly.*) It is Proserpina's! (*Turning to* OLD MAN *again.*) You found this near an opening in the ground?

OLD MAN

Yes. In fact it was close to where we are now standing. But you can see for yourself that there is no opening now.

CERES

(*Angrily striking at earth with her staff.*) Ungrateful land! You have robbed me of my dearest possession. I made you fertile so that you could produce much grain. I saw that the sun shone on you by day and that the rains watered your soil. But no more shall my favors be bestowed on you. That is my promise. Henceforth I shall spend all my days and nights in grieving for my lost Proserpina, my beloved daughter.

(*Lights darken. When they come on* CERES, OLD MAN *and* LITTLE GIRL *have left stage.* NARRATOR *is standing there.*)

NARRATOR

Ceres kept her word. No more was there prosperity on the land. Misfortune followed misfortune. Crops failed because the sun did not shine and the rains did not fall. Seeds were planted only to be stolen by the birds. Ploughs broke because the earth was too hard for them to go through. And soon the whole earth looked desolate. Ceres still mourned for her daughter.

(*Lights darken.* NARRATOR *leaves. When lights come on* CERES *is seated onstage. She is gazing straight ahead with unseeing eyes. A procession of people come in and kneel before her. A* YOUNG MAN *speaks.*)

YOUNG MAN

Ceres, Goddess of the Earth! We beseech you to give once more to the earth the fertility it used to enjoy.

CERES

(*Sternly.*) I have spoken! Never again will the earth receive my favors.

WOMAN

Ceres, beloved Goddess of the Earth! Our children are dying from starvation. Will you not help us?

CERES

I, too, have lost my child. I shall not forgive the earth.
(*The people all arise and walk sadly and slowly away.* ARETHUSA *enters and kneels before* CERES.)

ARETHUSA

May I speak to you, O Goddess Ceres? I am Arethusa, a woodland nymph and I bring you news of great importance.

CERES

You may speak, Arethusa.

ARETHUSA

This is not my land, O Goddess, but I feel that I must speak for it. The land did not open of its own accord to swallow your daughter. It was forced to.

CERES

Forced to! Who could force the land to disobey my wishes?

ARETHUSA

Listen to me, O Ceres, for I have seen your daughter, Proserpina.

CERES

(*Quickly.*) You have seen Proserpina? Where? And why has she not heard me and returned to me? Answer me quickly.

ARETHUSA

One day not so long ago I was returning from a hunt in the forest when an enemy of mine saw me and started to pursue me. I was sure I would be overtaken so I called on Diana, Goddess of the Hunt, to save me. She opened the earth so that I could descend and escape my pursuer.

CERES

I care not for the account of your escape. I care only to hear of my daughter. Where did you see her?

ARETHUSA

Patience, Ceres. I am coming to that. While I was passing through the earth I saw Proserpina. She is now the queen of Pluto, God of the Underworld, who rules over the dead. It is he who carried her off.

CERES

(*Covering her face with her hands for a moment then lifting her head again.*) I can hardly believe it. Tell me, how did she look?

ARETHUSA

Very sad.

CERES

There must be something I can do to release her. I shall seek help from Jupiter, ruler of all the Gods, to restore her to me. (CERES *turns and stretches her arms upward.*) O, Jupiter, ruler of all the Gods, hear my plea and restore my daughter to me.

(JUPITER *enters from direction where* CERES *is facing.* ARETHUSA *quietly leaves as he approaches.*)

172

PLAYS

JUPITER

Grieve no more, Ceres. I, Jupiter, have sent my messenger, Mercury, to the realms of Pluto to bring your daughter back to you. But there is one condition upon which your daughter's return depends.

CERES

And that condition?

JUPITER

She can return as long as she has not partaken of any food since she has been in Pluto's kingdom. If she has, she will have to remain with him.

(MERCURY *and* PROSERPINA *enter.*)

PROSERPINA

(*Running toward* CERES.) Mother, oh Mother!

CERES

(*Embracing* PROSERPINA.) My daughter! Once again you are with me.

JUPITER

(*To* MERCURY.) Were all the conditions met?

MERCURY

Not quite. Just before my arrival Proserpina had eaten some food.

PROSERPINA

(*Quickly.*) But very little. I was so very hungry that I ate but a few seeds from a pomegranate which Pluto offered me.

MERCURY

But Pluto has agreed to a compromise. Six months of the year Proserpina will be allowed to spend with her mother. The other six months must be spent with Pluto as his queen.

JUPITER

(*Turning to* CERES.) That you will have to agree to, Ceres.

CERES

(*Nodding her head slowly.*) I suppose there is no help for it. And the earth will be forgiven and made fertile during the months my daughter is with me. But while she is with Pluto, I shall grieve and the earth shall be barren.

JUPITER

Go, Mercury, and tell the mortals so that they can make their plans. They shall sow their seeds and their seeds will grow so that their harvest will be abundant. Let them gather the crops and store them in preparation for the days when Ceres again grieves for her daughter.

(*Lights darken. When they come on everyone has left stage and* NARRATOR *is standing there.*)

NARRATOR

And so did the ancient Romans explain the changing of the seasons. And thus they gave thanks to Ceres, Goddess of the Fields, for the fertility of their land and for the abundance of their harvests.

(*curtain*)

174

a thanksgiving nightmare

JANETTE WOOLSEY

CHARACTERS

FREDDIE BURNS	CRANBERRY
HIS MOTHER	PUMPKIN
HIS FATHER	CORN
TURKEY GOBBLER	APPLE
POTATO	NUT

COSTUMES

FREDDIE *wears pajamas,* MOTHER *and* FATHER *ordinary clothes. For the others make a cardboard cut-out and paint it to look like each character. It can be worn fastened to the shoulders and hanging down in the fashion of "sandwich men." The cut-outs can be as humorous and grotesque as possible. After all this is a nightmare! If the play is given in a school the making of the cut-outs could be an art project.*

PROPERTIES

A bed and any other pieces of bedroom furniture that are desired: a turkey drumstick for FREDDIE.

PRODUCTION NOTE

This play can be adapted for string marionettes or hand puppets. If this is done use only a bed and paint the other furniture on the background. Too much furniture may get in the way of amateur pupeteers and not allow them to move their marionettes or puppets freely.

TIME: *Thanksgiving evening.*

PLACE: *A bedroom.*

(*When curtain opens* FREDDIE *enters. He is wearing pajamas.*)

FREDDIE

(*Yawning widely.*) Oh, boy! Am I sleepy! And am I full, too! But how I love Thanksgiving. Turkey! Mashed potatoes! Cranberry sauce! Pumpkin pie! (*Rubbing his stomach.*) Yum! Yum! (*Holding up a drumstick and taking a bite.*) I sure hope Mom doesn't miss this drumstick. And I hope she doesn't discover that I ate another piece of pumpkin pie before I came to bed either. (*Yawning again.*) I guess I'll eat this in bed.

(FREDDIE *gets into bed. He starts to eat the drumstick but it soon gets to be too much effort and his hand finally falls down at his side and his eyes close.* FREDDIE *has fallen asleep.* CRANBERRY *enters stealthily walking on tiptoe. He comes over to* FREDDIE'S *bed and looks at him closely. Then he beckons toward the doorway. Background music of Saint-Saëns' "Danse Macabre" is heard playing softly. Keeping time to the music* TURKEY GOBBLER, PUMPKIN, POTATO, APPLE *and* NUT *march in. They join* CRANBERRY *at* FRED-

176

DIE's *bed. They shake their heads solemnly as they look down at him. Then they begin to march around his bed, stopping once in a while to shake their heads. After repeating this several times they come to the front of the stage. Music stops.*)

PUMPKIN

What do you think we ought to do with him?

CORN

I say, let's pop him. That's what he did to all my relatives. Popped them and ate them, that's what he did.

POTATO

I have a better idea. I say, let's mash him. When I think of all my relatives he ate I get ill. He loves mashed potatoes. "Put lots of gravy on them, please," he says. I think mashing is exactly what he needs.

NUT

Now I say, let's crack him. It gives me the shivers to think of how many of my relatives he ate.

PUMPKIN

My idea is to bake him. "What's Thanksgiving without pumpkin pie?" he said to his mother only yesterday. She was planning to have ice cream for dessert. But no! He had to have pumpkin pie.

APPLE

I wonder how he'd like to be peeled. Do you know how many of my relatives he's eaten? And not just today either. He eats them every day.

TURKEY GOBBLER

Now friends, wait a moment. You all have good ideas and I sympathize with every one of you. "Nothing like a good old drumstick," I've heard him say more times than I like to remember. But

177

don't you think we ought to give him a fair trial? Everybody deserves that.

CRANBERRY

Probably you're right but it's hard to want to be fair to him. Why, do you know today when he was eating some of my relatives he had the nerve to complain that they were too bitter. "Not enough sugar," he told his mother. (*Weeping.*) And they were the sweetest little berries I ever knew.

POTATO

(*Going over to console* CRANBERRY.) There, there. Don't cry. Mine didn't suit him either. He poured on gravy until they were completely smothered. "Makes them taste better," he said. You can imagine how that made me feel.

CORN

That seems to be a habit with him. Nothing suits him as it is. You should see him sprinkle salt and butter on my relatives after he's popped them.

PUMPKIN

Well, we're wasting time and we seem to be getting nowhere. Maybe Turkey Gobbler is right. Perhaps we should give him a fair trial.

NUT

Oh, all right. I'll agree too. But who will make a good judge?

CRANBERRY

I propose that Turkey Gobbler be the judge.

ALL TOGETHER

Yes. Yes. You be the judge, Turkey Gobbler!

TURKEY GOBBLER

If you're sure you want me. But the rest of you will be the jury and help me to decide his fate. Shall we hold the trial right here?

178

PUMPKIN

This seems as good a place as any.

TURKEY GOBBLER

Then everyone sit down, please. (*Everyone sits down in a semi-circle which half faces front and half faces the side, so that when* FREDDIE *is brought before the court he will not have his back to the audience.* TURKEY GOBBLER *sits in the middle,* POTATO *and* CRANBERRY *on either end and the others in between.* (*Solemnly.*) Let the prisoner be brought in.

    (CRANBERRY *and* POTATO *go over to the bed where* FREDDIE *is sleeping. They shake him hard.* FREDDIE *sits up in bed and rubs his eyes.*)

FREDDIE

(*Sleepily.*) Wh-what is it? (*Suddenly realizing what he is looking at.*) Wh-wh-who are you? (*Frightened.*) Wh-what do you want?

POTATO

(*Solemnly.*) Freddie Burns, get up right away.

FREDDIE

No. I don't want to. Go away, please. I don't know who you are.

CRANBERRY

(*Sternly.*) Freddie Burns, get out of that bed!

FREDDIE

(*Trying desperately not to act afraid.*) Oh, all right. But I don't have to, you know.

    (FREDDIE *gets cautiously out of bed.* POTATO *and* CRANBERRY *lead him over to where the others are sitting. He is placed in the center facing the others.* POTATO *and* CRANBERRY *take their seats.*)

179

FREDDIE

(*Really frightened now.*) Who are you? (*Looking at each one in turn.*) What do you want with me? How do you know my name?

TURKEY GOBBLER

Freddie Burns, we have brought you before us to give you a fair trial before we sentence you.

FREDDIE

Sentence me? What have I done?

TURKEY GOBBLER

You will know in due time. Are you prepared to tell the truth, the whole truth and nothing but the truth?

FREDDIE

I always tell the truth. (*Hesitatingly.*) That is *almost* always.
(*The rest of them shake their heads at this answer and whisper among themselves.*)

PUMPKIN

See? I knew it would be no use. How can we believe him?

FREDDIE

(*Eagerly.*) Oh, I'll tell you the truth. Honestly I will. Just ask me anything.

TURKEY GOBBLER

Very well. (*Suddenly.*) What day is this?

FREDDIE

(*Disgustedly.*) Thanksgiving Day, of course. I thought everyone knew that.

180

TURKEY GOBBLER

And what did you do today?

FREDDIE

Let's see. I ate my breakfast. Then I watched my mother stuff the turkey.

TURKEY GOBBLER

(*Interrupting.*) You did what?

FREDDIE

I watched my mother stuff the—(*Suddenly realizing what he's saying.*) stuff the—stuff the—

TURKEY GOBBLER

(*Sternly.*) Remember your promise! Stuff the what?

FREDDIE

(*Miserably.*) Stuff the turkey.
    (TURKEY GOBBLER *bows his head as if in grief. The others jump up and crowd around him patting him sympathetically. Then they all take their seats again.*)

TURKEY GOBBLER

(*Obviously making an effort to control himself.*) And-then-after-the-turkey-was-stuffed-what-did-you-do?

FREDDIE

(*Hanging his head.*) We put it in the oven.
    (PUMPKIN, CRANBERRY, APPLE, NUT, CORN *and* POTATO *point their fingers at* FREDDIE *and chant together.*)

ALL TOGETHER

Shame! Shame! Shame!

TURKEY GOBBLER

What happened after that?

FREDDIE

(*In a relieved tone.*) I went outdoors to play.

TURKEY GOBBLER

That's the first thing you've said in your favor. How long did you stay outdoors?

FREDDIE

Until my mother called me for dinner.

TURKEY GOBBLER

(*Sternly.*) And what did you have for dinner? Besides my poor brother, of course.

FREDDIE

(*Slowly.*) Mashed potatoes with gravy.

POTATO

(*Breaking into sobs.*) See? I told you so. (*Imitating* FREDDIE.) "Mashed potatoes with gravy. Please, lots of gravy. It makes the potatoes taste so good."

FREDDIE

(*Defiantly.*) Well, they're no good without it!
   (*The others run over to* POTATO *and console him and then take their places again.*)

TURKEY GOBBLER

(*To* FREDDIE.) Go on. What else did you have?

FREDDIE

Cranberry sauce. (*Quickly.*) But I didn't eat much of it. It was too bitter.

182

(CRANBERRY *bows his head and shakes all over as if he were crying hard. Then he raises his head and looks at* FREDDIE.)

CRANBERRY

Bitter, you say. Isn't it enough that you eat those dear little cranberries without insulting them by calling them bitter?

TURKEY GOBBLER

I don't suppose that was all you ate, was it?

FREDDIE

N-no. I had some pumpkin pie too.

PUMPKIN

(*Angrily.*) I knew he'd end up with that. I just knew it!

CORN

But he isn't through. I'm sure of that. (*To* FREDDIE.) Didn't you have something else?

FREDDIE

Well, not much. Only some apples and popcorn and nuts later on in the afternoon.

APPLE

He says, "Not much. Only some apples—"

CORN

"And popcorn—"

NUT

"And nuts." That's all he had!
    (*Everyone points his finger at* FREDDIE.)
Shame, shame, shame!

FREDDIE

(*Very frightened.*) What are you going to do to me?

183

TURKEY GOBBLER

We don't know yet. We'll have to talk it over first.

(TURKEY GOBBLER, POTATO, CRANBERRY, PUMPKIN, APPLE, CORN *and* NUT *all gather around and put their heads together. They whisper vehemently.* FREDDIE *stands there looking frightened. Finally everyone takes his seat again.*)

TURKEY GOBBLER

(*Solemnly.*) Freddie Burns, we have heard the evidence and have decided. We find the prisoner guilty!

FREDDIE

(*Crying.*) Oh, no! Please don't find me guilty! Please!

TURKEY GOBBLER

(*Pointing his finger at* FREDDIE.) And we sentence you to—roasting!

(*They all jump up and point their fingers at* FREDDIE.)

POTATO

To—mashing!

CRANBERRY

To—stewing!

PUMPKIN

To—baking!

CORN

To—popping!

APPLE

To—peeling!

NUT

To—cracking!

184

(*Then they all advance toward him.* FREDDIE *tries to get away from them. He runs around the room trying to escape and they follow him blocking his way to the door. They are all shouting,* "Roasting," "Mashing," "Stewing," "Baking," "Popping," "Peeling," "Cracking," *as they try to catch him. Suddenly he sees his way clear and jumps on the bed. He is yelling at the top of his voice.*)

FREDDIE

Mother! Daddy! Help! Help!

(*When he begins to yell all the others run off the stage in one direction as* FREDDIE'S MOTHER *and* FATHER *enter from the other. They rush over to his bed and* FATHER *begins to shake him.*)

MOTHER

Freddie! Freddie! Wake up!

FATHER

Stop yelling, son. Wake up. It's Mother and Dad.

(FREDDIE *finally sits up. He acts scared to death.*)

FREDDIE

Oh, Mom! Oh, Dad! Have they gone?

MOTHER

Has who gone, Freddie?

FREDDIE

The old Turkey Gobbler and his friends.

FATHER

(*Laughing.*) Sure. They've gone.

MOTHER

You've been having a nightmare, Freddie. (*Sternly.*) And I don't wonder. What's this in your hand? (*Pointing at the drumstick.*) And I noticed you ate another piece of pumpkin pie, too.

185

FREDDIE

(*Ashamedly.*) I guess maybe I ate too much.

FATHER

Well anyway, you know now that there's nothing wrong except too much Thanksgiving dinner. But back to sleep, son, and no more screaming.

MOTHER

(*Laughing.*) Please, no more! You really had me frightened.

FREDDIE

You weren't half as frightened as I was. I thought that Gobbler had me for sure. I'm not so sure I'll ever want any more turkey.

FATHER

You'll probably want some more by tomorrow. But go to sleep now.

MOTHER

And pleasant dreams.
(MOTHER *and* FATHER *leave.*)

FREDDIE

(*Sleepily.*) Good night. And I hope they're pleasant ones this time too.

(*curtain*)

POEMS FOR THANKSGIVING

november's gift

ALICE CROWELL HOFFMAN

November is a lady
   In a plain gray coat
That's very closely buttoned
   Up around her throat.

And after she's been roaming
   All around the town,
She reaches in her pocket,
   Deep, deep, down,

Then pulls out a present,
   And, with laughter gay,
Says to everybody,
   "Here's Thanksgiving Day!"

thanksgiving day in the morning

AILEEN FISHER

What is the place you like the best
Thanksgiving Day in the morning?
The kitchen! With so many things to test,
And help to measure, and stir with zest,
And sniff, and sample, and all the rest—
Thanksgiving Day in the morning.

What are the colors you like the most
Thanksgiving Day in the morning?
The colors of cranberries uppermost,
The pumpkin-yellow the pie tops boast,
The turkey-brown of a crispy roast—
Thanksgiving Day in the morning.

What are the sounds you think are gay
Thanksgiving Day in the morning?
The sizzly-sounds on the roaster-tray,
The gravy gurgling itself away,
The company-sounds at the door—hooray!
Thanksgiving Day in the morning.

thanksgiving time

UNKNOWN

When all the leaves are off the boughs,
   And nuts and apples gathered in,
And cornstalks waiting for the cows,
   And pumpkins safe in barn and bin;

Then Mother says: "My children dear,
   The fields are brown, and Autumn flies;
Thanksgiving Day is very near,
   And we must make Thanksgiving pies!"

thanksgiving day

LYDIA MARIA CHILD

Over the river and through the wood,
   To Grandfather's house we go;
     The horse knows the way
     To carry the sleigh
Through the white and drifted snow.

Over the river and through the wood—
   Oh, how the wind does blow!
     It stings the toes

And bites the nose,
As over the ground we go.

Over the river and through the wood,
To have a first-rate play.
Hear the bells ring,
Ting-a-ling-ding!
Hurrah for Thanksgiving Day!

Over the river and through the wood
Trot fast, my dapple-gray!
Spring over the ground
Like a hunting-hound!
For this is Thanksgiving Day.

Over the river and through the wood,
And straight through the barnyard gate.
We seem to go
Extremely slow—
It is so hard to wait!

Over the river and through the wood—
Now Grandmother's cap I spy!
Hurrah for the fun!
Is the pudding done?
Hurrah for the pumpkin pie!

goody o'grumpity

CAROL RYRIE BRINK

When Goody O'Grumpity baked a cake
The tall reeds danced by the mournful lake,
The pigs came nuzzling out of their pens,
The dogs ran sniffing and so did the hens,
And the children flocked by dozens and tens.
They came from the north, the east and the south
With wishful eyes and watering mouth,
And stood in a crowd about Goody's door,
Their muddy feet on her sanded floor.
And what do you s'pose they came to do!
Why, to lick the dish when Goody was through!
And throughout the land went such a smell
Of citron and spice—no words can tell
How cinnamon bark and lemon rind,
And round, brown nutmegs grated fine
A wonderful haunting perfume wove,
Together with allspice, ginger and clove,
When Goody but opened the door of her stove.
The children moved close in a narrowing ring,
They were hungry—as hungry as bears in the spring;
They said not a word, just breathed in the spice,
And at last when the cake was all golden and nice,
Goody took a great knife and cut each a slice.

the landing of the pilgrim fathers

FELICIA DOROTHEA HEMANS

The breaking waves dashed high
  On a stern and rock-bound coast,
And the woods against a stormy sky
  Their giant branches tossed.

And the heavy night hung dark
  The hills and waters o'er,
When a band of exiles moored their bark
  On the wild New England shore.

Not as the conqueror comes,
  They, the true-hearted, came,
Not with the roll of stirring drums,
  And the trumpet that sings of fame;

Not as the flying come,
  In silence and in fear—
They shook the depths of the desert's gloom
  With their hymns of lofty cheer.

Amidst the storm they sang,
  And the stars heard and the sea!
And the sounding aisles of the dim wood rang
  To the anthems of the free!

The ocean-eagle soared
  From his nest by the white waves' foam,
And the rocking pines of the forest roared—
  This was their welcome home!

There were men with hoary hair
   Amidst that pilgrim-band;
Why had they come to wither there,
   Away from their childhood's land?

There was woman's fearless eye,
   Lit by her deep love's truth;
There was manhood's brow serenely high,
   And the fiery heart of youth.

What sought they thus afar?
   Bright jewels of the mine?
The wealth of seas, the spoils of war?
   They sought a faith's pure shrine!

Ay, call it holy ground,
   The soil where first they trod!
They have left unstained what there they found—
   Freedom to worship God!

the pilgrims came

ANNETTE WYNNE

The Pilgrims came across the sea,
And never thought of you and me;
And yet it's very strange the way
We think of them Thanksgiving Day.

We tell their story, old and true,
Of how they sailed across the blue,
And found a new land to be free
And built their homes quite near the sea.

Every child knows well the tale
Of how they bravely turned the sail,
And journeyed many a day and night,
To worship God as they thought right.

The people think that they were sad,
And grave; I'm sure that they were glad—
They made Thanksgiving Day—that's fun—
We thank the Pilgrims, every one!

all in a word

AILEEN FISHER

T for time to be together,
   turkey, talk, and tangy weather.

H for harvest stored away,
　　home, and hearth, and holiday.

A for autumn's frosty art,
　　and abundance in the heart.

N for neighbors, and November,
　　nice-things, new-things to remember.

K for kitchen, kettles croon—
　　with kith and kin expected soon.

S for sizzles, sights, and sounds,
　　and something-special that abounds.

That spells THANKS . . . for joy of living
and a jolly good Thanksgiving.

if i were a pilgrim child

ROWENA BENNETT

If I were a Pilgrim child,
　　Dressed in white or gray,
I should catch my turkeys wild
　　For Thanksgiving Day.
I should pick my cranberries
　　Fresh from out a bog,
And make a table of a stump
　　And sit upon a log.
An Indian would be my guest

And wear a crimson feather,
And we should clasp our hands and say
  Thanksgiving grace together.
But I was born in modern times
  And shall not have this joy.
My cranberries will be delivered
  By the grocery boy.
My turkey will be served upon
  A shining silver platter.
It will not taste as wild game tastes
  Though it will be much fatter;
And, oh, of all the guests that come
  Not one of them will wear
Moccasins upon his feet
  Or feathers in his hair!

a good thanksgiving

MARIAN DOUGLAS

Said old Gentleman Gay, "On a Thanksgiving Day,
If you want a good time, then give something away."

So he sent a fat turkey to Shoemaker Price,
And the shoemaker said, "What a big bird! How nice!
And, since a good dinner's before me, I ought
To give poor Widow Lee the small chicken I bought."

"This fine chicken, oh see!" said the pleased Widow Lee,
"And the kindness that sent it, how precious to me!
I would like to make someone as happy as I—
I'll give Washwoman Biddy my big pumpkin pie."

198

"And oh, sure!" Biddy said, " 'Tis the queen of all pies!
Just to look at its yellow face gladdens my eyes!
Now it's my turn, I think, and a sweet ginger cake
For the motherless Finnigan children I'll bake."

"A sweet cake, all our own! 'Tis too good to be true!"
Said the Finnigan children, Rose, Denny, and Hugh;
"It smells sweet of spice, and we'll carry a slice
To poor little lame Jake, who has nothing that's nice."

"Oh, I thank you, and thank you!" said little lame Jake,
"Oh, what a beautiful, beautiful, beautiful cake!
And oh, such a big slice! I will save all the crumbs,
And will give 'em to each little sparrow that comes!"

And the sparrows they twittered, as if they would say,
Like old Gentleman Gay, "On a Thanksgiving Day,
If you want a good time, then give something away!"

father, we thank thee

RALPH WALDO EMERSON

For flowers that bloom about our feet,
    Father, we thank Thee,
For tender grass so fresh and sweet,
    Father, we thank Thee,
For the song of bird and hum of bee,
For all things fair we hear or see,
Father in heaven, we thank Thee.

For blue of stream and blue of sky,
   Father, we thank Thee,
For pleasant shade of branches high,
   Father, we thank Thee,
For fragrant air and cooling breeze,
For beauty of the blooming trees,
Father in heaven, we thank Thee.

For this new morning with its light,
   Father, we thank Thee,
For rest and shelter of the night,
   Father, we thank Thee,
For health and food, for love and friends,
For everything Thy goodness sends,
Father in heaven, we thank Thee.

thanks

NORMAN GALE

Thank you very much indeed
River, for your waving reed;
Hollyhocks, for budding knobs;
Foxgloves, for your velvet fobs;
Pansies, for your silky cheeks;
Chaffinches, for singing beaks;
Spring, for wood anemones
Near the mossy toes of trees;
Summer, for the fruited pear,
Yellowing crab, and cherry fare;
Autumn, for the bearded load,

Hazelnuts along the road;
Winter, for the fairy tale,
Spitting log and bouncing hail.

But, blest Father, high above,
All these joys are from Thy love;
And Your children, everywhere,
Born in palace, lane, or square,
Cry with voices all agreed,
"Thank You very much indeed."

thanksgiving

AMELIA E. BARR

FIRST PUPIL

Have you cut the wheat in the blowing fields,
    The barley, the oats, and the nodding rye,
The golden corn and the pearly rice?
    For the winter days draw nigh.

SECOND PUPIL

We have reaped them all from shore to shore,
And the grain is safe on the threshing floor.

THIRD PUPIL

Have you gathered the berries from the vine,
    And the fruit from the orchard trees?
The dew and the scent from the roses and thyme,
    In the hive of the honey bees?

201

FOURTH PUPIL

> The peach and the plum and the apple are ours,
> And the honeycomb from the scented flowers.

FIFTH PUPIL

> The wealth of the snowy cotton field
>   And the gift of the sugar cane,
> The savory herb and the nourishing root—
>   There has been nothing given in vain.

SIXTH PUPIL

> We have gathered the harvest from shore to shore,
> And the measure is full and brimming o'er.

ALL

> Then lift up the head with a song!
>   And lift up the hand with a gift!
> To the ancient giver of all
>   The spirit in gratitude lift!
> For the joy and the promise of spring,
>   For the hay and the clover sweet,
> The barley, the rye and the oats,
>   The rice and the corn and the wheat,
> The cotton and sugar and fruit,
>   The flowers and fine honeycomb,
> The country so fair and so free,
>   The blessings and glory of home.

merry autumn days

CHARLES DICKENS

We hail the merry Autumn days
    When leaves are turning red;
Because they're far more beautiful
    Than anyone has said;
We hail the merry harvest time,
    The gayest of the year;
The time of rich and bounteous crops,
    Rejoicing and good cheer.

autumn fires

ROBERT LOUIS STEVENSON

In the other gardens
    And all up the vale,
From the autumn bonfires
    See the smoke trail!

Pleasant summer over
    And all the summer flowers,
The red fire blazes,
    The gray smoke towers.

203

Sing a song of seasons!
Something bright in all!
Flowers in the summer,
Fires in the fall!

singing the reapers homeward come

UNKNOWN

Singing, the reapers homeward come, Io! Io!
Merrily singing the harvest home, Io! Io!
Along the field, along the road,
Where autumn is scattering leaves abroad,
Homeward cometh the ripe last load, Io! Io!

Singers are filling the twilight dim
With the cheerful song, Io! Io!
The spirit of song ascends to Him
Who causeth the corn to grow.
He freely sent the gentle rain,
The summer sun glorified hill and plain,
To golden perfection brought the grain, Io! Io!

Silently, nightly, fell the dew,
Gently the rain, Io! Io!
But who can tell how the green corn grew,
Or who beheld it grow?
Oh! God the good, in sun and rain,
He look'd on the flourishing fields and grain,
Till they all appear'd on hill and plain
Like living gold, Io! Io!

we plough the fields

MATTHIUS CLAUDIUS

We plough the fields, and scatter
  The good seed on the land,
But it is fed and watered
  By God's almighty hand;
He sends the snow in winter,
  The warmth to swell the grain,
The breezes and the sunshine,
  And soft refreshing rain.

      All good gifts around us
      Are sent from heaven above;
      Then thank the Lord, O thank the Lord,
      For all His love.

We thank Thee, then, O Father,
  For all things bright and good,
The seed-time and the harvest,
  Our life, our health, our food;
Accept the gifts we offer,
  For all Thy love imparts,

And, what Thou most desirest,
Our humble, thankful hearts.

All good gifts around us
Are sent from heaven above;
Then thank the Lord, O thank the Lord,
For all His love.

come ye thankful

GEORGE J. ELVEY

Come, ye thankful people, come,
Raise the song of harvest home:
All is safely gathered in,
Ere the winter storms begin;
God, our Maker, doth provide
For our wants to be supplied:
Come to God's own temple, come,
Raise the song of harvest home.

All the world is God's own field,
Fruit unto his praise to yield;
Wheat and tares together sown,
Unto joy or sorrow grown:
First the blade, and then the ear,
Then the full corn shall appear:
Lord of harvest, grant that we
Wholesome grain and pure may be.

psalm 95

THE BIBLE

O come, let us sing unto the Lord:
Let us heartily rejoice in the strength of our salvation.
Let us come before his presence with thanksgiving.
And show ourselves glad in him with psalms.
For the Lord is a great God,
And a great King above all gods.
In his hands are all the corners of the earth:
The strength of the hills is his also.
The sea is his, and he made it:
And his hands prepared the dry land.
O come, let us worship and bow down:
Let us kneel before the Lord our maker.
For he is the Lord our God:
And we are the people of his pasture and the sheep of his hand.

psalm 100

THE BIBLE

Make a joyful noise unto the Lord, all ye lands.
Serve the Lord with gladness; come before his presence with sing-
      ing.
Know ye that the Lord he is God: it is he that hath made us, and

not we ourselves: we are his people, and the sheep of his pasture.

Enter into his gates with thanksgiving, and into his courts with praise: be thankful unto him and bless his name.

For the Lord is good; his mercy is everlasting; and his truth endureth to all generations.

psalm 136

THE BIBLE

O give thanks unto the Lord; for he is good:
For his mercy endureth forever.
O give thanks unto the God of gods:
For his mercy endureth forever.
O give thanks to the Lord of lords:
For his mercy endureth forever.

To him who alone doeth great wonders:
For his mercy endureth forever.
To him that by wisdom made the heavens:
For his mercy endureth forever.
To him that stretched out the earth above the waters:
For his mercy endureth forever.
To him that made great lights:
For his mercy endureth forever.
The sun to rule by day:
For his mercy endureth forever.
The moon and stars to rule by night:
For his mercy endureth forever.

O give thanks unto the God of heaven:
For his mercy endureth forever.

be thou praised

ST. FRANCIS
(*from The Mirror of Perfection*)

Be Thou praised, my Lord, of our Sister, Mother Earth,
    which sustains and hath us in rule,
    and produces divers fruits with colored flowers and herbs.

Praise ye and bless my Lord, and give Him thanks,
    and serve Him with great humility.

though our mouths were full of song

THE HEBREW MORNING SERVICE
(*from The Hebrew Prayer Book*)

Though our mouths were full of song as the sea,
and our tongues of exultation as the multitude of its waves,
and our lips of praise as the wide-extended firmament;
though our eyes shone with light like the sun and the moon,
and our hands were spread forth like the eagles of heaven,
and our feet were swift as hinds,

we should still be unable to thank thee and bless thy name,
O Lord our God and God of our fathers,
for one thousandth or one ten thousandth part
of the bounties which thou hast bestowed
upon our fathers and upon us.

a thought

ROBERT LOUIS STEVENSON

It is very nice to think
The world is full of meat and drink,
With little children saying grace
In every Christian kind of place.

child's grace

FRANCES FROST

I give thanks for the lovely-colored year,
For the marigold sun and slanting silver rain,
For feathery snow across the hemlock hills,
For the sailing moon twelve times grown full again.

I give thanks for my family; Father, Mother,
And all the happy things we do together;
For understanding, laughter, and for love
Strong and warm in any kind of weather.

210

table blessing

LEW WALLACE
(*from Ben Hur*)

Father of all—God!
What we have here is of Thee;
Take our thanks and bless us,
That we may continue
To do Thy will.

a child's grace

ROBERT BURNS

Some hae meat and canna eat,
   And some wad eat that want it;
But we hae meat and we can eat,
   And sae the Lord be thankit.

GAMES FOR THANKSGIVING FUN

GAMES

JANETTE WOOLSEY

hunt the turkeys

PROPERTIES: *Turkey decals pasted on small pieces of cardboard.*
Before the guests arrive, hide the turkeys around the room.
When you are ready for this game tell the guests that somehow all
the Thanksgiving turkeys have gotten away and you've been told
they are hiding in this room. The children try to find the turkeys,
and as each child finds one he brings it to the host who keeps track
of how many each child finds. The game is over when all the turkeys
are accounted for and the winner is the one who found the most.

corn hunt

PROPERTIES: *As many kernels of corn as desired.*
Before the children arrive at the party, hide as many kernels of
corn as desired around the room. When the game starts, the children try to find the corn in a given length of time. The one finding
the most is the winner.

215

follow the string

PROPERTIES: *A favor for every child; lots of string.*

This game is a good "ice breaker" to help children feel at ease when they first come to your party. Hide Thanksgiving favors all over the room. Attach strings to them and wind the strings all around various pieces of furniture. Each child is given the end of a string when he comes in, and as soon as everyone is there they all begin to follow their strings until the favors are found. Be sure you don't wind the strings around breakable objects!

corn straws

PROPERTIES: *A cupful of freshly-made popcorn and a hatpin.*

This is played like the old game of Jackstraws. The first player is given a cup of popcorn which he turns out on the table. Then he tries to remove each piece of popcorn by spearing it with the hatpin. He must be careful not to move any other piece. If he does, he forfeits his turn to the next player. Score is kept and the popcorn which was removed is returned to the cup each time so that each player has the same amount with which to play. The player having the highest score after every one has had a turn is the winner.

spearing popcorn

PROPERTIES: *A hatpin for each player; a bowl of freshly-made popcorn for every two players.*

216

Each player is given a hatpin, and two players are assigned to each bowl of popcorn. Then each player tries to spear the popcorn one piece at a time. At a given time the person who has removed the most corn is the winner.

pin the tail on the turkey

PROPERTIES: *A large drawing of a turkey which is pinned onto a sheet fastened onto the wall; as many turkey tails as players.*

Each player is blindfolded and turned around several times. Then he is faced toward the turkey with one of the turkey tails in his hand. He must then try to pin the tail on the turkey. After everyone has had a try, the winner is declared to be the one who has put it in the most ridiculous place.

pitching the corn into a bowl

PROPERTIES: *Six kernels of corn; one bowl.*

The bowl is placed in the center of the room. Each player, from a given spot, tries to pitch six kernels of corn, one at a time, into the bowl. The game may continue for several rounds and the score is kept. The child having the highest score at the end of the game is declared the winner.

stringing the cranberry

PROPERTIES: *Lots of cranberries; string and darning needle for each child.*

Place the cranberries in several bowls so that all the children playing will have equal access to them. Give each child a darning needle and a string of the same length. The idea is to make a necklace of cranberries. The one who finishes first is declared the winner.

where is the turkey?

PROPERTIES: *A small toy turkey.*

One person is "It" and leaves the room. The rest decide on a hiding place for the turkey. "It" comes back and begins to look for the turkey. If he is not close, the rest of the children begin to shiver and act cold. As he gets closer to it they begin to act warm. When he is very close they begin to fan themselves and act as though they are very hot. After the turkey is found, another child is "It."

corn, corn, who has the corn? (1)

PROPERTIES: *One kernel of corn.*

The players all sit around in a circle. Each one clasps his hands together but leaves a small opening between his thumbs. One child is "It." In his clasped hands he has a kernel of corn. He goes

218

around the circle and pretends to drop the corn into the hands of each child. Into one of them he actually does drop the corn, but continues around until he has completed the circle. Then he says, "Corn, corn, who has the corn?" All the children try to guess and the one who has the corn pretends to guess too. The child who guesses right is "It" next time.

corn, corn, who has the corn? (2)

PROPERTIES: *One kernel of corn.*
In this variation of the corn game all the players sit in a circle. But this time they pass the corn from one to the other being very careful not to let it be seen. One person finally keeps the corn but pretends to pass it. "It" who is standing in the middle of the circle tries to guess who has the corn. As soon as he does the person who kept the corn is "It" next time.

dance with the indian

PROPERTIES: *Broom; paper bag; colored paper for feathers.*
This game requires a little preparation beforehand. Fit a paper bag over a broom. Draw a face on it and dab some paint on it so it will look like Indian war paint. Make a headband with colored feathers and fit it on the top of the bag. Now you are ready for your game. An uneven number of children have to play this. Have some slips of paper ready which are all blank except one. On this slip write the word, "Indian." The child who draws this slip has to dance the first dance with the "Indian." All the others choose partners. When the music begins everyone dances. When the music stops everyone must change partners. The child with the "Indian"

219

passes it to someone else who, in turn, tries to pass it on. No one can refuse to take the "Indian" but they can try to get rid of it as soon as possible. Whoever is holding the "Indian" when the music begins again has to dance that dance with the "Indian."

a thanksgiving mix-up

This is really the old fashioned game of Fruit Basket. Instead of fruit, however, the name of anything connected with a Thanksgiving dinner is used. The children all sit around in a circle. The person who is "It" gives each one a name such as, "Turkey," "Mince Pie," "Cranberry Sauce" etc. Then "It" begins by saying, "Turkey and Mince Pie." Immediately those two have to change places. "It" continues this as long as he wants to and then he says, "The dining room table tipped over." Then everyone has to exchange chairs and "It" scrambles for a chair, too. The person left without a chair is "It" the next time. The same name may be given to more than one person. It makes exchanging chairs a little more exciting.

the indian chief says—

This is patterned after the old game, Simon Says. The child who is chosen to be "Indian Chief" stands in front of the others. He orders the others what to do and each time follows the order himself. Each time he gives an order he must say, "The Indian Chief says." If he just says, "The Chief says," even though he carries out the order himself the others must not obey. If anyone does, he is out of the game. The game continues until several are eliminated and then a new "Indian Chief" is chosen. The orders could go like this, "The Indian Chief says, 'Waggle your fingers' "; "The Indian Chief says, 'Give a war whoop' "; "The Chief says, 'Nod your heads.' "

priscilla, where art thou?

PROPERTIES: *Two blindfolds.*

Two children are selected—one to be John Alden and the other to be Priscilla Mullins. The other children sit around the room or they may stand to form a large circle. John and Priscilla are then blindfolded and led into the circle and placed at opposite sides. They are then turned around several times so that their sense of direction is confused. Then John says, "Priscilla, where art thou?" "Here, John," Priscilla answers. John must then try to find Priscilla. She moves around too trying to stay out of his way. But everytime he calls, "Priscilla, where art thou?" she must answer even if she is close to him. After John has caught Priscilla two other children are chosen to play.

thanksgiving dinner

Everyone is seated in a circle. The first person begins by saying, "At my Thanksgiving dinner I ate turkey." The second player says, "At my Thanksgiving dinner I ate turkey and mashed potatoes." The third player says, "At my Thanksgiving dinner I ate turkey, mashed potatoes and cranberry sauce." The game continues with each player adding something which would be part of a Thanksgiving dinner. The idea of course is that everything that anyone says must be repeated in exactly the same order by each succeeding player. If anyone makes a mistake he is out of the game. The game continues until there is just one person left.

pumpkin relay race

PROPERTIES: *Two Pumpkins; two wooden spoons.*

The players are divided into two teams and each team is divided into two parts. Half stand on each side of the room, facing each other. The first one on each team at a given signal has to roll a small pumpkin with a wooden spoon across the room to where the other half of his team is. The first player at that end then takes the spoon and rolls it back to the other side. The game is won by the side whose players finish first.

feather relay

PROPERTIES: *Two feathers.*

The players are divided into two teams. Each team is divided into two parts. Half stand at each side of the room facing each other. The first player on each side is given a feather which he must blow to the other half of his team. The first player on that side blows it back to the starting point. The game is won by the team whose last player finishes ahead of the other team. Of course one strict rule is "No hands." If the feather falls to the floor the player has to blow it from that position.

corn race (1)

PROPERTIES: *A kernel of corn for each player; two bowls.*

The players are divided into two teams. Each player is given a kernel of corn which he places on the back of his left hand. If the player happens to be left-handed he must place it on his right hand. With his hand with the corn on it extended in front of him and his other hand in back of him, he must try to reach the bowl at the opposite side of the room and deposit his corn in it. If his corn falls off before he reaches the bowl he is out of the game. After all the players have had a turn the side wins which has the most corn in the bowl.

corn race (2)

PROPERTIES: *Two bowls; as many knives as players; six kernels of corn for each player.*

The players are divided into two teams. Each player is given a knife and six kernels of corn. The players of each team are lined up one behind the other. The bowls are placed at the opposite end of the room. The players all place the corn on their knives. The first player on each team starts out. He must cross the room and drop his corn into the bowl. If he loses any corn on the way he cannot pick it up. The winning team is the one which has the most corn in its bowl after all the players have had their turn.

relay corn race

PROPERTIES: *Two kernels of corn and two toothpicks.*

The players are divided into two teams and each team is divided into two parts. Each half stands at the opposite side of the room facing its teammates. The first player on each team has a kernel of corn which he pushes across the room with a toothpick to his teammate on the opposite side of the room. Then that player takes over and pushes the corn back to the second player who is opposite him. The game continues until all the players on one team have had a chance to play. That team is declared the winner.

224

passing the corn

PROPERTIES: *Twenty kernels of corn; four bowls.*

The children are divided into two teams and the children on each team stand one in back of the other. The first and last child on each team holds a bowl. The kernels of corn are placed in the bowl held by the child at the head of each line. The idea is to pass the corn, a kernel at a time, back over the shoulders until it has reached the last child who puts it into his bowl. Everyone must look straight ahead and is not allowed to look over his shoulder at the person to whom he is passing the corn. If anyone drops a kernel he calls out, "Stop" and everyone on his team has to stop right in the middle of what he is doing and hold that position. When the player finds the corn he has dropped he takes his place in the line. He calls out, "Start" and everyone continues as before. The game is over when one team finally gets all the kernels into the bowl the last child is holding.

a memory test by sight

PROPERTIES: *A paper and pencil for each child; a cranberry; a toy turkey or a picture of one; a Pilgrim doll (a candle made in a Pilgrim mold will do); a potato; an onion; a piece of pumpkin; a walnut; an Indian doll or headdress; an apple; a date; a piece of celery; a small calendar with the Thanksgiving date encircled; blindfolds for each child.*

In one room arrange the above articles on a table. Then blindfold the children and lead them into the room where the articles are. Remove the blindfolds and allow them to look at the table for about two minutes. Then they must go back to the other room and write down everything they have seen. The winner is the child who remembers the most.

a memory test by feeling

A variation of the Memory Test By Sight is to leave the contestants blindfolded and let them feel the objects. You can use the same objects as listed above with the exception of the calendar. After each child has felt the objects they go into another room and write down all they remember. The winner is the child who has the most right.

cranberries

PROPERTIES: *A bowl and a box of cranberries; pencil and paper for each child.*

Place the contents from a box of cranberries into a bowl. The children must then try to guess how many cranberries there are. Each one writes the number he has guessed and his name on a slip of paper. The host collects the slips and reads the answers. The one guessing nearest the correct number is the winner.

count the corn

PROPERTIES: *A jar and plenty of corn; pencil and paper for each child.*

A variation of Cranberries. Fill a jar with kernels of corn and let the children guess how many are in it. Each one writes his guess on a slip of paper with his name and hands it to the host. The one nearest to the right number is the winner.

twenty questions

A variation on the well known game of "Twenty Questions" is that every object chosen to be guessed must be someone or something connected in some way with Thanksgiving. "It" says he is thinking of something. Then the questioning goes around the circle in turn until the object or person is guessed in twenty questions or less. All questions must be asked so that they can be answered by "yes" or "no." Suppose for example "It" has selected the *Mayflower* for his object. The questioning might go something like this.

Question	Answer
1. Is it alive?	No
2. Is it something that was made?	Yes
3. Does it exist now?	No
4. Was it made a long time ago?	Yes
5. Was it something back in Pilgrim days?	Yes
6. Could I carry it?	No
7. Was it something very large?	Yes
8. Was it made of metal?	No
9. Was it made of wood?	Yes
10. Was it a Pilgrim house?	No
11. Could it be moved?	Yes
12. Could it move by itself?	Yes
13. Was it a ship?	Yes
14. Was it the *Mayflower?*	Yes

a thanksgiving word game

PROPERTIES: *A paper and pencil for each child.*

Give each child a paper and pencil. Each one is told to write the word *Thanksgiving* at the top of the page. Now each one should try to make as many words as possible from it. The one who has the longest list in a given time is the winner. Here are some of the words that can be made: tag, tags, tan, tang, tank, task, than, thank, thanks, thin, thing, think, this, ting, tink, hag, hake, hang, hank, has, hint, his, hit, anti, ask, ash, nag, nigh, ninth, kin, king, kit, kith, knight, knit, sag, saint, sang, sank, sat, satin, saving, shag, sight, sign, sin, sing, sink, skat, snag, stag, stain, stang, sting, gag, gain, gait, gang, gas, gash, gig, gin, giving, gnash, gnat, ink, inn, insight, itch, its, van, vanish, vast, visit, vista.

a scrambled thanksgiving dinner

PROPERTIES: *A paper and pencil for each child.*

Give each child a paper and pencil. Have written on each paper the list which is in the left hand column. The first one to unscramble the dinner wins.

Nupmipk Epi	Pumpkin Pie
Tarso Yurket	Roast Turkey
Rarybecrn Ascue	Cranberry Sauce
Shadem topato	Mashed Potato
Fungstif	Stuffing
Shaqus	Squash
Ronc Dabre	Corn Bread
Necim Ipe	Mince Pie
Tibgel Vargy	Giblet Gravy
Daltes Tuns	Salted Nuts

228

a thanksgiving bingo game

PROPERTIES: *Toy turkey; cranberry; onion; potato; corn; piece of pumpkin; apple; nut; date; candy; olive; roll; picture of Pilgrim; picture of ship; feather; paper and pencil for each child.*

Place the sixteen objects listed above on a table. Label them all so the children will have the correct spelling. Give each child a large sheet of paper which has been divided into sixteen squares. Tell the children they are to copy the names of the objects onto each square in whatever order they prefer. The host has written the names onto separate slips which have been placed in a hat. After the children have finished copying the words onto the squares the host draws his slips from the hat and reads them off. As he does this each child draws a cross through that name on his sheet. The one who gets four names in a row calls, "Bingo," and wins the game. The finished square is illustrated on the next page.

Turkey	Cranberry	Roll	Potato
Celery	Onion	Date	Nut
Pilgrim	Corn	Olive	Feather
Ship	Pumpkin	Candy	Apple

RECIPES FOR THANKSGIVING GOODIES

thanksgiving goodies

ELIZABETH HOUGH SECHRIST

Oh, some like magic made by wands,
And some read magic out of books,
And some like fairy spells and charms
But I like magic made by cooks!
Rowena Bennett
(*from "Thanksgiving Magic"*)

Thanksgiving is definitely a feast day, and everyone enjoys eating special goodies on that day. Why not surprise
your mother on this holiday by helping her with the preparations
for the feast? Try out some of these recipes on your family. Or, if
you are going to entertain some of your school friends on or near
the Thanksgiving holiday, you may discover what fun it is to have
an old-fashioned taffy-pull, or to make candied apples. Boys as
well as girls can make cooking fun. The recipes chosen here, from
the cookie place-cards to cornmeal pancakes suggested for Thanksgiving breakfast, are the do-it-yourself variety that you CAN DO!

233

cookie place-cards for thanksgiving dinner

1 package prepared cookie mix *water*
1 cup confectioners sugar *food coloring*

Prepare cookie mix (or your own favorite cookie recipe). Roll out on floured board to ⅛ inch thickness. Use turkey-shaped cookie-cutter if available, if not, cut out dough in 2″ by 3″ oblongs. Bake in oven. (See directions for temperature and time on package.) When cool, write names of the dinner guests on the cookies with colored icing. To make icing, add just enough cold water to sifted confectioners sugar to make it possible to force through a pastry tube. Be very careful not to make it too moist. Add few drops of food coloring of any desired color.

apple snow

1 cup grated apple *¾ cup powdered sugar*
2 egg whites

Place all ingredients in mixing bowl and beat with electric mixer until stiff enough to stand up in firm peaks. This may be served with fruit Jello or soft custard, or plain with whipped cream topping.

234

apple crisp

4 cups sliced pared apples   ½ cup sugar
½ cup flour   ½ cup butter
                   ¼ cup hot water

Pare and slice the apples and put them into a buttered baking dish. Pour the hot water over them. In a bowl, cream the sugar and flour into the butter to form crumbs. Sprinkle crumbs over the apples and bake in 400° oven for 35 to 45 minutes. Test with fork to see if apples are tender.

deep dish apple pie

1 package pie crust mix   1 cup sugar
6 or 7 apples   1 tablespoon melted butter
                   ½ teaspoon cinnamon

Prepare pie crust according to directions on package. Butter individual baking dishes. Scrub apples and slice in thin slices without paring. Add sugar, cinnamon and melted butter and stir well. Place mixture in the baking dishes until ¾ full. Roll out pastry and cut desired size to fit over baking dishes. Press edges firmly down over rim of each baking dish. Slash crust in center to let steam escape. Bake in 350° oven for about 40 minutes.

easy pumpkin pie

1 package prepared pie crust
    mix
1¾ cups canned pumpkin
1¾ cups milk
½ teaspoon salt
2 eggs

⅔ cups brown sugar
2 tablespoons granulated sugar
1 teaspoon cinnamon
½ teaspoon nutmeg
½ teaspoon ginger
¼ teaspoon cloves (if desired)

Mix the canned pumpkin, milk, salt and eggs with beater. Add the sugar and spices and mix well. Prepare pastry by following directions on pie crust mix. Line 9-inch pie plate with the crust and pour pumpkin mixture into it. Bake in 425° oven 45 to 55 minutes. The custard is done when a table knife, inserted in the side of filling, comes out clean. Do not overbake.

mince pie roll

1 package prepared pie crust
    mix

1 pint mince meat
1 chopped apple

Prepare the pie crust according to directions on the package. Roll it to ⅛ inch thickness in a long rectangle. Mix the chopped apple with the mince meat and spread it on the pie dough. Roll as for jelly roll, pinching the ends together so the filling will not escape. Place in well-greased pan with the folded side down. Bake in 350°

oven for about 40 minutes. When cool, sprinkle with powdered sugar. Slice like jelly roll and serve hot or cold.

graham cracker pie

14 graham crackers	1 teaspoon baking powder
1 cup sugar	½ cup chopped nuts
¼ teaspoon salt	3 eggs
	1 teaspoon vanilla

Mash crackers with rolling-pin and put into mixing bowl. Add sugar, salt, baking powder, and chopped nuts. Separate eggs and beat yolks until foamy. Add vanilla and yolks to crumb mixture. Fold in stiffly-beaten egg whites. Pour into buttered 9-inch pie plate. Bake in 350° oven for 35 minutes. Top with sweetened whipped cream.

fried pies

1 package prepared pie crust mix	water (as directed on package) thick sweetened applesauce

Make pie crust according to directions on package. Divide into two portions and roll out on floured board, one portion at a time. Roll pastry ⅛ inch thick and cut into circles 3 or 4 inches in diameter. Place 1 tablespoon applesauce in center of each circle. Moisten edges with cold water and fold over, making a semicircle. Press edges together with a fork, making sure the pastry edges are all closed. Fry in deep fat, 375°, until golden brown. Drain. When cold sprinkle with powdered sugar.

crullers

½ cup butter
1 cup sugar
2 eggs, well-beaten
3½ teaspoons baking powder

¼ teaspoon nutmeg
½ teaspoon salt
3½ cups sifted flour (approx.)
1 cup milk

Cream butter and sugar, add eggs. Mix. Add 1 cup flour, baking powder, salt and nutmeg. Blend. Then add alternately the remaining flour and milk until stiff enough to roll out. Roll ½ inch thick. Cut with round cookie-cutter. Cut thimble-sized hole in center of each cruller. Fry in deep fat, 375°, and turn several times while they are frying. Sprinkle with powdered sugar when cool.

applesauce cake

¼ cup butter or margarine	½ teaspoon nutmeg
1 cup sugar	¼ teaspoon cloves
2 cups flour	¼ teaspoon allspice
2 eggs	1 teaspoon soda
½ teaspoon salt	1 cup applesauce
1 teaspoon cinnamon	1 cup raisins

1 cup chopped nuts (*if desired*)

Cream shortening and sugar together and add beaten eggs. Dissolve soda in applesauce and add. Sift all the dry ingredients together in a separate bowl. Add to first mixture and mix well. Bake in well-greased loaf pan for one hour in 350° oven.

rice krispies cookies

⅔ cup shortening	1 cup flour
1 egg	¼ teaspoon salt
1 cup light corn syrup (*or maple syrup*)	¼ teaspoon soda
	2 cups Rice Krispies

Cream shortening and add beaten egg and syrup. Sift dry ingredients together and add to first mixture. Mix. Add Rice Krispies and mix well. Drop in small mounds on lightly-greased cookie-sheet and bake at 350° for ten minutes.

chocolate wheaties

2 7-ounce packages semisweet chocolate chips
4 cups Wheaties

Melt chocolate in double boiler. Cool but don't let it harden. Add the wheaties and stir until well-coated. Drop by spoonfuls onto waxed paper and chill in refrigerator. If desired, 1 cup of peanuts or other nuts may be used with 3 instead of 4 cups Wheaties.

easy nut cookies

⅔ cup sweetened condensed milk   3 tablespoons cocoa
1 cup chopped nuts (peanuts may be used)

Blend the cocoa well with the condensed milk. Stir in nuts and mix well. Drop by spoonfuls onto well-greased cookie-sheet and bake in 350° oven for fifteen minutes.

salted peanut cookies

1 cup shortening
2 cups brown sugar
2 eggs
1 cup sour milk (or buttermilk)
2 cups flour

2 cups rolled oats
1 cup Wheaties
1 teaspoon salt
1 teaspoon soda
1 cup chopped salted peanuts

Mix shortening, sugar and eggs together. Add milk. (If sour milk or buttermilk is not available, add 1 tablespoon vinegar to sweet milk.) Sift flour and add salt, soda, rolled oats and Wheaties. Chop the salted peanuts, not too finely, and add. Drop by spoonfuls onto greased pan. Bake in 400° oven for about 12 minutes or until brown.

candied apples

8 large apples and 8 wooden
    skewers
2 cups granulated sugar
1 cup brown sugar

⅔ cup corn syrup
¼ lb. (or one stick) butter
1 cup cream or evaporated
    milk

Wash and chill apples. Cook remaining ingredients in kettle large enough to keep mixture from boiling over. After mixture boils, stir to prevent scorching. When syrup forms a hard ball when dropped into cold water, remove from heat and set aside to cool. Insert skewers into apples and twirl them into cooling candy mixture until well-covered. Dip into ice water to harden candy, then place on waxed paper.

popcorn balls

3 cups granulated sugar	1 tablespoon vinegar
1 cup light syrup	4 tablespoons butter
1 cup water	3½ cups freshly-made popcorn, well-salted.

Place the popcorn in a large bowl. Remove any unpopped pieces. Cook sugar, syrup, water and vinegar together until a thread spins from the edge of the spoon when tested. Add butter last and pour the mixture slowly over the popcorn. When cool enough to handle, shape into balls. (Various types of cold cereals may be substituted for popcorn.)

"mosies"

4 cups brown sugar	½ cup water
1 tablespoon butter	1 cup chopped nuts

Cook the sugar, butter and water until the syrup forms a hard ball when dropped into cold water. Remove from heat and beat until creamy, like fudge. Add chopped nuts. Pour into buttered pans. When cool, cut into squares.

molasses chewies

½ cup molasses   2 tablespoons butter
½ cup corn syrup   1 tablespoon vinegar
2 cups shredded coconut

Put all ingredients except coconut into saucepan. Cook over low heat, stirring until boiling stage is reached. Boil until a sample dropped in cold water becomes brittle. Remove from heat and add coconut. Drop in small mounds on waxed paper.

molasses taffy

1 cup molasses   2 teaspoons vinegar
1 cup granulated sugar   1 tablespoon butter
¼ teaspoon baking soda

Cook all above ingredients except the soda in 2-quart saucepan. Keep heat low and stir until sugar is dissolved. Increase heat and boil, stirring occasionally, until hard ball is formed when syrup is dropped into cold water. Add soda and remove from heat. Pour out on well-buttered platter. As it cools, keep pulling the edges, with fingers, toward center so the edges will not harden before the center. By the time it is cool enough to pull, the taffy will have been pushed into a ball in center of the platter. The fingers must be well-buttered to pull the taffy. It should be pulled until it begins to harden, then stretched to form long ropes about ½ inch wide. Cut into one-inch pieces and wrap in waxed paper.

penuchi

2 cups brown sugar	pinch salt
½ cup evaporated milk	1 teaspoon vanilla
2 tablespoons butter	1 cup broken nut meats

Cook milk and sugar together over low heat until soft ball forms when tested in cold water. Add butter and cool slightly, then add milk, salt, vanilla and nuts. Beat until creamy and pour into buttered pan. Cut into squares when cool.

uncooked fondant

⅔ cup condensed milk	1 teaspoon vanilla
4½ cups confectioners sugar (sifted)	1 teaspoon almond extract

Add the sugar gradually to the condensed milk until well-blended. Add the flavorings. Knead with hands until creamy. Cover with a damp towel and keep in refrigerator 24 hours before using. May be used to stuff dates, to form into candies with nuts or maraschino cherries, etc.

chocolate fondant

1 can sweetened condensed milk   1 chocolate bar (*milk chocolate,*
½ lb. dot chocolate   *two-ounce size*)
1 cup chopped nuts

Melt chocolate in double boiler. Stir in can of condensed milk. Let stand in refrigerator overnight, to thicken. Add nuts and form into small balls. Place on waxed paper or well-buttered dish and re-chill.

stuffed dates

Dates may be stuffed with either of the two fondants above, or with nuts. A pitted date stuffed with a whole walnut and rolled in granulated sugar is *my* favorite!

spiced nuts

1½ cup nuts (whole)	½ cup cornstarch
2 tablespoons cold water	1 teaspoon nutmeg
1 egg white	2 teaspoons cinnamon
2 cups confectioners sugar	2 teaspoons ginger
2 teaspoons salt	2 teaspoons cloves

Add the cold water to the slightly beaten egg white. Using a fork, coat each nut with egg mixture. Sift all the dry ingredients together and roll the nuts in a portion of this mixture until well-coated. Put half the remaining portion in a shallow pan until bottom of pan is covered. Place the nuts well apart in the pan and cover with the remainder of the spice mixture. Bake in 250° oven for about two hours. Shake in a coarse strainer to remove excess spice mixture from the nuts.

stuffed celery

crisp fresh celery	⅛ teaspoon pepper
1 cake cream cheese, 3-ounce size	⅛ teaspoon paprika
¼ teaspoon salt	2 or 3 drops Worcestershire sauce (if desired)
mayonnaise	

Wash celery and place in ice water and keep in refrigerator until well-chilled. Drain. Cream the cheese until smooth and add the seasoning and enough mayonnaise to make spreading easy. Fill celery stalks. Chill.

celery trunks

Fill celery stalk with filling (as above) and press together with a second stalk of equal size. Match stalks together in this way and stand upright to resemble trees. Be sure to leave some of the celery leaves at top of stalk.

relish dish

radishes	*cauliflower*
olives	*carrots*
celery	

Any or all of these raw vegetables may be used to make an attractive relish dish for the Thanksgiving table. Clean and chill them. Pare the carrots and cut into thin strips so they will curl when chilled. Separate the flowerets of the cauliflower. The celery may be cut into thin strips and dropped into ice water until the strips curl. Radish roses can be made by carefully cutting the skin back to form rose petals. The main thing to remember in preparing the relish dish is to have the vegetables fresh, crisp, and ice-cold.

For a round relish dish, try putting celery trunks in the center and surround them with flowerets, radish roses, olives and carrot curls. For a long dish use stuffed celery, olives, radish roses. Or celery sticks, carrot sticks, olives and radish roses. Better still, use your own ideas!

sweet potato balls

2 cups hot mashed sweet potatoes
¼ cup pineapple juice

1 cup crushed cornflakes
marshmallows

Add pineapple juice to the hot mashed sweet potatoes and beat until smooth. Using one marshmallow for each as a center, form balls of the sweet potato mix. Then roll in crushed cornflakes until well-coated. Bake in 350° oven for 25 to 30 minutes.

corn pudding

2 cups canned creamed corn
1 tablespoon melted butter
½ teaspoon salt

2 teaspoons baking powder
1 tablespoon cornstarch
2 eggs, well-beaten

½ cup milk

Mix in bowl in the order given. Pour into greased casserole and bake at 325° for 50 minutes.

cornmeal pancakes

2 cups yellow cornmeal	1 teaspoon baking soda
½ cup white flour	1 egg
pinch salt	1 tablespoon melted butter
	2 cups buttermilk

Sift the cornmeal, flour, salt and soda together. Break the whole egg into it, add melted butter, then add buttermilk a little at a time until just well-blended but not smooth. Bake on hot griddle and serve hot with butter and honey. These are a treat for breakfast on Thanksgiving morning!

ABOUT THE AUTHORS

ELIZABETH HOUGH SECHRIST became interested in writing for children while she was a Children's Librarian in Bethlehem, Pennsylvania. Each year she was asked by boys and girls, teachers and librarians, for information on Christmas in other lands. Because of the lack of material, she began to collect and write on the subject herself, and the resulting book, *Christmas Everywhere,* has been popular in schools and libraries for many years.

After nine years' experience in Bethlehem and Pittsburgh libraries, Mrs. Sechrist gave up her work to devote her time to writing, editing and lecturing on children's books—and incidentally, to keeping house. At Spring Meadow Farm in York County, Pennsylvania, where she and her husband live, a collection of cookbooks is conspicuous on the shelves along with those on birds, animals and furniture. Spring Meadow Farm is a lively place with its sheep, lambs, cocker spaniels, cats and kittens, ducks and geese.

And yet amidst all this activity, Mrs. Sechrist finds time to write books—although she claims the days are never long enough!

JANETTE WOOLSEY is a librarian at the Martin Memorial Library in York, Pennsylvania. One summer her library program was a marionette theater, and it was during this time that she became interested in play production and writing. She and the children wrote the plays and presented them to a capacity audience each week. Miss Woolsey is a graduate of Middlebury College, Pratt Institute and Columbia University. She started her library career as Children's Librarian at Ohio University. She lives in York, and devotes much of her free time to lecturing about children's books and storytelling.